SHRUBS

THE NEW

GLAMOUR

PLANTS

Bob Hyland ⁄ Guest Editor

FOR THE
ADVANCE-
MENT OF
BOTANY
AND THE
SERVICE OF
THE CITY

BROOKLYN
BOTANIC
GARDEN
PUBLICATIONS
· MCMXCIV ·

Janet Marinelli
EDITOR

Bekka Lindstrom
ART DIRECTOR

Stephen K-M. Tim
VICE PRESIDENT, SCIENCE & PUBLICATIONS

Judith D. Zuk
PRESIDENT

Elizabeth Scholtz
DIRECTOR EMERITUS

Handbook #141

Copyright © Autumn1994 by the Brooklyn Botanic Garden, Inc.

BBG gardening guides are published quarterly at 1000 Washington Ave., Brooklyn, NY 11225

Subscription included in Brooklyn Botanic Garden membership dues ($25.00 per year)

ISSN 0362-5850 ISBN # 0-945352-86-7

PRINTED IN KOREA

Table of Contents

Perennials in Disguise?

BY BOB HYLAND

Shrubs are more than "foundation plants" intended to camouflage unsightly walls or fences. They are the "bones" of our gardens, providing the framework for all the other plants. But for too long shrubs have taken a back seat to more glamorous perennials and glitzy annuals. This handbook is designed to finally give these indispensable plants their due. Shrubs are destined to become the new glamour plants in the American garden.

It wasn't easy to select this sampler of shrubs. Although scores of shrubs are featured in the pages that follow, this is by no means the definitive shrub encyclopedia; hundreds of additional plants could easily have been included, given the space. You'll notice, for starters, that hollies, rhododendrons and conifers are not included; it was, alas, necessary to draw the proverbial line somewhere.

I feel fortunate to have had bicoastal gardening experiences in the East (the mid-Atlantic, Northeast, Southeast and south Florida) as well as the West (northern and southern California). Based on my familiarity with and love of plants from so many different areas I've encouraged contributors to this handbook to discuss shrubs without the usual bias toward one region of the country found in most gardening books. (Let's not beat around the bush — there's more to America than the temperate East Coast!) Among the featured shrubs are both deciduous and evergreen types suited not only to temperate but also desert, Mediterranean and subtropical climates. A variety of forms and sizes are also included to fit the scale of any garden. Shrubs were chosen for their exceptional flower power (size, color and fragrance), handsome foliage, ornamental interest in at least two seasons and insect and disease resistance. Native shrub species are included where appropriate for the growing number of gardeners interested in native plants and natural habitat gardening.

Whether in our gardens or in larger public landscapes, well-chosen shrubs offer shape, color, texture and often fragrance. Massed together, shrubs provide screening and privacy. They are invaluable in mixed borders with perennials, bulbs and other ephemeral plantings; they also make natural supports for sprawling vines. For gardeners with limited space, there are shrubs that grow well in containers on patios, decks and terraces. Shrubs are also essential for attracting birds, butterflies and other wildlife to our gardens.

We demand an awful lot from shrubs, yet often we don't spend the time to choose as wisely and plant as carefully as we do with other vegetation. This handbook will help you select the right shrub for the right place, and plant it properly so that it gets off to a good start.

In small gardens, shrubs such as the California lilac, *Ceanothus* 'Julia Phelps', pictured at left, can be trained to grow against a wall.

I gratefully acknowledge the contribution of Bob Hays, propagator at Brooklyn Botanic Garden, who helped to compile the collection of featured shrubs, write plant profiles and gather photos. Expert horticulturists and educators around the country reviewed our shrub selections and helped us tailor a diverse mix. They also contributed the articles on planting, pruning and designing with shrubs and had a hand in the regional shrub recommendations at the back of this book. Many thanks to the following people:

Michael Dirr, University of Georgia, Athens
Harrison Flint, Purdue University, West Lafayette, Indiana
Bill Frederick, Private Gardens, Inc., Hockessin, Delaware
Kent Gullickson, Oakland, California
Ed Hasselkus, University of Wisconsin at Madison
Allen Howard, Fairchild Tropical Garden, Miami, Florida
Mary Irish, Desert Botanical Garden, Phoenix, Arizona
Kris Jarantoski, Chicago Botanic Garden
Scot Medbury, University of California at Berkeley
J.C. Raulston, North Carolina State University Arboretum, Raleigh
Bill Thomas, Longwood Gardens, Kennett Square, Pennsylvania

I hope this handbook introduces you to some new shrubs and reacquaints you with old favorites. Most of all, I hope you're inspired to go out and plant shrubs. Together, maybe we can even spur the formation of an American Shrub Association — those perennial plant enthusiasts and their Perennial Plant Association need some competition!

WHAT'S IN A NAME?

Throughout this handbook you'll find lists of "cultivars" for most shrubs. A cultivar, short for "cultivated variety," is a plant with one or more unique characteristics that distinguish it from other members of the same species. The species are the plants with the two-part Latin names. The cultivars are the plants with a Latin name followed by another name in single quotation marks; the name that follows the Latin name often describes the cultivar's unique characteristic. (The handful of plants with three-part Latin names are varieties that occur naturally in the wild.) A cultivar may differ from the species in size, flower color, leaf color or cold hardiness. It may originate from an unusual plant found in the wild, be developed by hybridization or be selected from plants cultivated in gardens or nurseries.

Japanese barberry, *Berberis thunbergii*, shown below, and the three cultivars pictured on the bottom of the page are graphic illustrations of how

Berberis thunbergii

cultivated varieties differ from the species and from each other. The species has medium-green leaves, sometimes tinged with purple. 'Atropurpurea', bottom left, has glossy, deep-purple leaves. The leaves of 'Rose Glow', bottom center, are mottled with light and dark shades of purple. Those of 'Golden Ring', bottom right, have bright green edges.

B.t. 'Atropurpurea'

B.t. 'Rose Glow'

B.t. 'Golden Ring'

THE NEW SHRUB-PLANTING GOSPEL

BY J.C. RAULSTON

D URING THE PAST DECADE, extensive research by plant scientists has resulted in the revision of many of the traditional "gospel truths" about planting practices, particularly shrub planting practices. For example, gardeners were — and often still are — routinely advised to amend the soil in their garden — that is, to change its physical properties (which is very different from fertilization, which changes its chemical properties) to make it more suitable to the new shrub. Yet amending the soil often has no value, or in some cases, detrimental effects. For instance, adding sand to "increase soil aeration and drainage" rarely does. In most cases, and particularly in clay soils, it actually decreases aeration and drainage and is not recommended.

Adding organic matter is also questionable in many cases. Organic matter is the result of the breakdown of living tissue as organisms die and decay. Breakdown is the key word — the organic matter ultimately disintegrates into water and carbon dioxide. The levels of organic matter in soils are controlled by the temperature, aeration and moisture levels of a given climate and soil type, and cannot be changed on a permanent basis in a garden. In other words, adding peat or other organic matter has a temporary effect that will disappear with time, although the speed at which it will disappear is quite variable. In a cool northern location with low aeration and moisture it may remain for many years; whereas in warmer, wetter Florida, it will completely disappear within months.

Unlike the annual vegetable or flower beds where amendments can be added easily each growing season, shrub plantings are relatively permanent. It makes far more sense to choose a shrub on the basis of its adaptability to the site than to try to make the site suitable to the shrub. So the first axiom for proper planting is to choose the right shrub for your site.

When you're ready to plant, carefully remove the growing medium from the outside of the roots. Then work the roots into the new soil with your fingers.

THE RIGHT PLANT FOR THE SITE

Hardiness — the ability to tolerate cold winters — is the major criterion used to determine a plant's adaptability to a particular location. The U.S. Department of Agriculture and others have divided the country into "hardiness zones," and plants are assigned a range of zones in which they have proven reliably hardy. However, low winter temperature is only one of many climatic factors to which a shrub must be adapted, including out of season frosts, heat and rainfall.

What's more, there are two major — and very different — environments to consider: not only the above-ground world of climate but also the underground root zone. Half of a plant is underground, and conditions in this subterranean environment must also match the needs of the shrub you choose.

Your soil's physical properties are the most critical to consider when choosing a shrub, as they are difficult to change. The size of particles (ranging from extremely fine in clays to coarse in sands and gravels) and their relative proportions are used to classify soils into various categories: sandy loams, silty clays and so on. As soils become coarser in texture, the proportion of open pore space between the solid particles increases. This open pore space contains the air (oxygen) and water essential to good plant growth.

Your soil's chemical properties revolve around the relative availability of a group of 14 to 18 "essential elements" required by all plants, including the familiar nitrogen, phosphorus and potassium. The relative acidity or alkalinity (the pH) of your soil is also important because it determines which essential elements are available to your plants, and to what degree. Neutral to slightly

9

acidic soils (pH 5.5 to 7.0) are usually best. Because deficient elements can be added, and pH can be adjusted up or down with commercial fertilizers, the initial chemical properties of your soil are less critical than its physical characteristics in appropriate plant selection.

It is possible to find excellent shrubs for all areas of the country that will grow well in virtually any kind of existing soil without difficult and expensive modifications — a far easier and more ecological approach than trying to "fit the soil to the plant."

There are a few instances in which amending the soil may be advisable. For example, shrubs in the Ericaceae or heath family (*Arctostaphylos*, azaleas, *Enkianthus, Gaultheria, Kalmia, Leiophyllum, Leucothoe, Oxydendrum, Pieris, Rhododendron, Vaccinium* and *Zenobia*, among others) have relatively specific soil requirements. They generally require fairly acidic soils with excellent aeration, constant moisture and high levels of organic matter, and so you may want to create a raised planting bed of mostly organic material. Or, no matter what shrub you're planting, if the "soil" in your garden is highly artificial — the contractor has bulldozed any existing topsoil, say, and left mostly subsoil and builder rubble in its place — you should consider buying a good quality topsoil and creating a new planting bed.

BARE ROOT, BALLED AND BURLAPPED OR CONTAINER GROWN?

Shrubs are generally available in three different forms: bare root, balled and burlapped and container grown. In years past, many shrubs were sold as dormant, bare-root stock — that is, the plants were field-grown in soil and dug bare root in winter when dormant. To prevent drying, they were packaged with the roots in various paper or plastic packages filled with a loose, moist medium.

If purchased while the plant is dormant and the roots are still moist and healthy, bare-root shrubs are likely to do as well as any. The roots are directly in contact with the new soil and grow quickly throughout a uniform environment. In recent years with the advent of container-grown plants, bare-root plants have declined in market share but are still an excellent way to buy plants.

Balled and burlapped (B&B) shrubs are also field-grown in soil. But they are dug with a quantity of the soil around the intact roots, and then tightly wrapped in burlap or other material for transport and handling. For the same size specimen, B&B plants are often more expensive than bare-root plants, as the digging process involves more expensive hand labor, and shipping and handling the heavy soil adds to costs as well. Today, with the shift to container-grown

Left: Burlap or other wrapping materials should be removed before planting.
Center and right: Pass up plants that are rootbound or have girdling roots.

plants, which eliminates the digging costs, fewer B&B shrubs are available. Larger specimen plants, and certain slow-growing shrubs such as boxwood and yew, are still commonly sold B&B. They generally establish well.

However, if the soil in the root ball and the soil in the planting bed are very different, it may help to partially "bare root" the outside of the root ball to get some of the roots in direct contact with the new soil. Remove the burlap or other wrapping material just before you are ready to plant.

These days, the vast majority of shrubs are container grown. The new soilless growing mediums offer excellent drainage and aeration, which allows the plants to be grown much faster. What's more, because the expense of hand digging is eliminated, these plants are often relatively inexpensive.

It might seem at first that container-grown specimens would have great advantages, as no roots are removed or disturbed by digging or packaging. In general, this may be true, but there are circumstances in which they are difficult to establish. Plants that are rootbound — that is, their roots have completely filled the container — can be particularly problematic. This is because the new, coarse-textured soilless mixes often used in container production have been engineered for maximum pore space to provide optimum aeration for the fastest possible plant growth. On the down side, this also means that such mixes hold very little water, and an overgrown plant can completely remove all the water from the container medium in a matter of hours on a sunny or windy day. In a nursery with automated irrigation systems, containers are watered several times a day. But if a rootbound specimen is planted as-is in a garden, there will be no "connection" between the roots and the soil in the new bed; under such circumstances, plants sensitive to desiccation can dry out and die quickly.

"Butterflying" of container-grown plants is often recommended to get roots in contact with the soil. This involves making a vertical cut through the root system from the bottom of the container to about two-thirds the height of the roots, followed by a second cut at a right angle to the first. The four root segments are then spread out and soil is worked into the roots. Although this practice at first glance appears sensible and puts roots in contact with soil, it also severs most of the roots into many small spaghetti-like pieces no longer attached to the plant!

Gardeners often create their own problems by buying the biggest plant possible. The best container plants are those that have not become overgrown and rootbound — often smaller is better.

PLANTING TIPS

If it isn't advisable to amend the soil, then what do you do when it's time to get down to the actual planting? Spade or till the existing soil well to the depth of the root ball or container. The width of the planting hole is especially important: two to three times wider than the root ball is a good rule of thumb.

Add fertilizer to provide the optimum pH and essential elements as indicated by soil tests or general recommendations for your area.

During planting, the most important goal is to get the new plant's roots into the new soil environment as quickly as possible so the plant will suffer as little stress from water loss as possible.

Remove as much of the growing medium from the outside of the roots as you can. Then proceed by working the roots into the new soil with your fingers to get them directly in contact with "real" soil.

Always plant the shrub with the roots at the same height as they were in the container or at the nursery, or slightly higher in heavy soils. Water immediately. Shield the plant from full sun and wind for a week or two with a translucent cloth or paper cover and continue to water every few days until it no longer wilts.

If any branches have been broken or damaged during transportation and planting, they should be pruned back to healthy wood. Because shrubs are normally shorter at planting time than trees, they rarely need staking.

Finally, it's a good idea to mulch the planting bed to conserve moisture, but don't overdo it. During the last ten years a deep-mulching fad has taken the gardening world by storm; mulch is often applied as much as a foot deep around trees and shrubs. This can damage trunk bark and prevent healthy oxygen exchange with the soil. Normally, two to four inches of mulch is quite adequate.

LANDSCAPING WITH SHRUBS

BY WILLIAM H. FREDERICK, JR.

ONE OF THE GREATEST JOYS of a garden is having a series of pleasing effects that change with the seasons. These effects can be in the form of flowers, foliage color or texture, interesting bark, berries or fragrance. Shrubs, even more than trees and groundcovers, fill this role most admirably and with a minimum of maintenance.

In my Delaware garden, for example, fragrant wintersweet (*Chimonanthus praecox*) ushers in the new year, bearing fragrant yellow flowers on warm days in January. It is followed by the spidery yellow blossoms of witchhazel (*Hamamelis mollis* 'Pallida') in February and March. The sparkling of catkins on willows, *Salix gracilistyla* (gray) and *S. g. melanostachys* (black), and Harry Lauder's walking stick (*Corylus avellana* 'Contorta') carry the show into early April.

A background of shrubs in the author's garden offers seasonal effects.

It is at this moment that spring explodes into bloom, with such treats as the pendulous green-yellow blossoms of winterhazels (*Corylopsis pauciflora* and *C. spicata*), which contrast with the warm lavender blossoms of Korean rhododendron (*Rhododendron mucronulatum*). Early May brings the captivating fragrance of spice viburnum (*Viburnum carlesii*). The many colorful hues of tree peonies such as the magnificent black pirate (*Paeonia* 'Black Pirate'), featuring maroon blooms with yellow centers, follow later in the month. The elegant white cones of oakleaf hydrangea (*Hydrangea quercifolia*) appear in June.

July's fireworks include the colorful wands of butterfly bush (*Buddleia davidii*) in blue, lavender and maroon shades as well as white. The flower-tipped branches nod in the summer breezes, and are a magnet for multicolored butterflies. August would be a dull month without the newer hybrid rose-of-sharons (*Hibiscus syriacus*). They are unaffected by heat and drought. 'Diana' is waxy white; 'Blue Bird' is an attractive shade of blue with white flower parts. All summer long the maroon foliage of purpleleaf smokebush (*Cotinus coggygria* 'Purpureus') puts on a fine performance. This shrub makes a fine backdrop for the September-blooming, mauve-pink *Lespedeza thunbergii* 'Gibraltar'.

Hardy-orange (*Poncirus trifoliata*) produces striking miniature yellow oranges on green, thorny stems in October, which contrast happily with the clusters of small, lavender berries on beautyberry (*Callicarpa dichotoma*). The latter is effective through early freezes and can be counted on for a good November show.

The red fruits of winterberry (*Ilex verticillata* 'Winter Red' or *I.* 'Scarlett O'Hara') are especially effective in December when grown with the dark-green-leaved meserve hollies, such as *Ilex* x *meserveae* 'Blue Maid'.

WHERE TO PUT SHRUBS

How do you integrate these plantings of seasonal interest into your garden design? There are really two answers to this question.

In the first place, they should be planted where they naturally will do well from a cultural standpoint and won't require coddling. This means you must choose shrubs matched carefully to your hardiness zone (see the hardiness zone map on page 106) and the light, moisture, wind and soil conditions of your site. From a design point of view, shrubs simply should be planted where they will be enjoyed the most. Put a planting of shrubs with interesting bark, colorful twigs and winter berries near a window, where you can see it during the winter months. Locate those with fragrant blossoms near an entrance or along a path or walkway that is frequently travelled.

The blossoms of April-, May- and early-June-blooming shrubs arrive at a time when those of us in cold climates are starved for color. This is an event of sufficient significance that we are willing to walk to more remote parts of the garden to enjoy them. The same is true of shrubs with blooms or berries in the fall. Once the dog days of summer have departed and brisk fall weather arrives, we are once again inspired to stroll and enjoy the farther reaches of our gardens and the shrubs flowering and fruiting there. Shrubs at their peak interest from late June through early September, a time when we want to enjoy our gardens from a comfortable chair in a shady location, are best planted near a deck, screened porch, patio or pool.

In what other ways are shrubs useful?

The lavender flower spikes of chastetree stand out against the deep purple leaves of a copper beech.

CONTRASTING LEAF AND TWIG TEXTURES

To create especially lively plantings, I recommend combining shrubs with contrasting forms and textures. An example of such a planting would be Scotch broom (*Cytisus scoparius*), which has very fine twigs and a vertical habit, and bayberry (*Myrica pensylvanica*), which has broad leaves and a very moundy habit. Concentrate fine-textured plants near the centers of interest on your property (such as a doorway or garden feature) and broader-leaved plants farther away.

TYING PLANTINGS TOGETHER

Shrubs are especially important tools of the garden designer as they provide the glue that holds mixed plantings (trees, shrubs, groundcovers, perennials, grasses) together. This is because of the horizontal effects they can provide. Such effects can come, for example, from the horizontal branching habits of such larger shrubs as burning bush (*Euonymus alatus*) or doublefile viburnum

(*Viburnum plicatum tomentosum*). Because groundcovers also form horizontal lines, a similar effect can be produced by massing one kind of low-growing shrub as a groundcover. Good candidates are Wilton's juniper (*Juniperus horizontalis* 'Wiltonii'), spreading plum yew (*Cephalotaxus harringtonia pedunculata*) and crimson pygmy barberry (*Berberis thunbergii* 'Crimson Pygmy').

COLOR COMBINATIONS

One of the greatest challenges of garden design is to provide wonderful color combinations. Shrubs are a major player in this respect. I would feel lost without shrubs with foliage in three colors: blue-green, maroon and yellow-green. They are useful mixers, pulling other colors together. Among the best examples are:

Blue-Green Foliage:

Tamarisk (*Tamarix ramosissima*)

Leatherleaf Mahonia (*Mahonia bealei*)

Wilton's Juniper (*Juniperus horizontalis* 'Wiltonii')

Maroon Foliage:

Smokebush (*Cotinus coggygria* 'Purpureus')

Japanese Barberry (*Berberis thunbergii* 'Atropurpurea')

Virginia Sweetspire (*Itea virginica* 'Henry's Garnet' — fall only)

Yellow-Green Foliage:

Old Gold Juniper (*Juniperus* x *media* 'Old Gold')

Variegated Thorny Elaeagnus (*Elaeagnus pungens* 'Maculata')

Yellow-green foliage is an especially good mixer for red-yellow-orange combinations. The blue-greens and maroons work equally well with the pink-lavender-purple and the red-yellow-orange combinations.

I do have one caveat. Reading descriptions of the shrubs featured in this book is enough to make you want to plant one of each. This, of course, would create the effect of a zoo and must be resisted if you want to compose a successful picture. With rare exceptions, shrubs with colorful blooms or fruits are more effective in groups of three or more than when planted as single specimens. It is instructive to drive through suburban neighborhoods during April and observe the spottiness caused by one or two bright yellow forsythias in each garden. In your mind's eye, bring all of these spots of color together in a solid sweep of, say, 25 plants — what a glorious sight that would be!

Generally speaking, I like to think of trees as three-dimensional structural elements in garden design; of groundcovers as two-dimensional space shapers; and of shrub compositions as the real engines driving seasonal effects. Shrubs, therefore, deserve our strong attention when we design our gardens.

GROWING SHRUBS IN CONTAINERS

BY KENT GULLICKSON

AESTHETICS AND RESTRICTED SPACE are the most common reasons for growing shrubs in containers. Millions of people, especially in urban situations, do all their gardening in pots — and quite successfully, too, as the rooftops and balconies of big cities from Manhattan to Rome attest. Whatever the reason for growing plants in pots, container gardening often results in a relationship between gardener and plant that rather resembles that between a parent and a young child. Potted plants remain dependent for water and feeding long after individuals of the same species will have gained at least a measure of self-sufficiency in the ground. Container-grown plants do not have access to the same reserves of nutrients and water that shrubs planted out have; interruption of the supply of either is stressful for plants; and like people, plants under stress often perform poorly.

But growing shrubs in pots also has its advantages. Perhaps the most compelling reason to put up with the added effort of it all is simply that in pots you're able to grow things that otherwise wouldn't survive in the garden. For example, our garden is located in a "banana belt" in the foothills of Oakland, California, and is essentially frost-free most winters. Our biggest problem isn't the cold, it's the soil — heavy, thick, dark, sticky clay with a six-inch overlay of good soil in the best spots. I have a fondness for aloes, especially some of the ones that get big, and I've lost some to cold, but more to wet feet. In any case, if they're in

CHOICE SHRUBS FOR POT CULTURE

COMMON NAME	BOTANICAL NAME
Flowering Maple	*Abutilon* x *hybridum*
Agapetes	*Agapetes serpens*
Japanese Barberry	*Berberis thunbergii*
Angel's Trumpet	*Brugmansia versicolor*
Bottlebrush	*Callistemon citrinus*
Sasanqua Camellia	*Camellia sasanqua*
Red Cestrum	*Cestrum elegans* 'Smithii'
Mexican-orange	*Choisya ternata*
Orchid Rockrose	*Cistus* x *purpureus*
Tartarian Dogwood	*Cornus alba* 'Sibirica'
Cotoneaster	*Cotoneaster congestus* 'Likiang'
Burkwood Daphne	*Daphne* x *burkwoodii*
Garland Daphne	*Daphne cneorum*
Enkianthus	*Enkianthus campanulatus*
Red Escallonia	*Escallonia rubra*
Harry Lauder's Walking Stick	*Corylus avellana* 'Contorta'
Burning Bush	*Euonymus alatus*
Box-leaf Euonymus	*Euonymus japonicus* 'Microphyllus'
Variegated Euonymus	*Euonymus japonicus* 'Albo-marginatus'
Dwarf Fothergilla	*Fothergilla gardenii*
Gardenia	*Gardenia augusta*
Hawaiian Hibiscus	*Hibiscus rosa sinensis*
Rose-of-Sharon	*Hibiscus syriacus*
Bigleaf Hydrangea	*Hydrangea macrophylla*
Oakleaf Hydrangea	*Hydrangea quercifolia*
Chinese Holly	*Ilex cornuta* 'Dazzler'
Mountain-laurel	*Kalmia latifolia*
New Zealand Tea	*Leptospermum scoparium*
Loropetalum	*Loropetalum chinense*
Mahonia	*Mahonia lomariifolia*
Pink Melaleuca	*Melaleuca nesophylla*
Greek Myrtle	*Myrtus communis*
Honeybush	*Melianthus major*
Heavenly-bamboo	*Nandina domestica*
Oleander	*Nerium oleander*
Delavayi Osmanthus	*Osmanthus delavayi*
Variegated Holly-leaf Osmanthus	*O. heterophyllus* 'Variegatus'
Photinia	*Photinia* x *fraseri*
Mountain Andromeda	*Pieris japonica*
Pittosporum	*Pittosporum tobira*
Cherry-laurel	*Prunus laurocerasus*
Indian Hawthorn	*Rhaphiolepis indica*
Rosemary	*Rosmarinus officinalis*
Variegated American Elderberry	*Sambucus canadensis* 'Variegata'
Japanese Skimmia	*Skimmia japonica*
Japanese Snowball	*Viburnum plicatum tomentosum* 'Mariesii'
Variegated Weigela	*Weigela florida* 'Variegata'

CHOICE SHRUBS FOR POT CULTURE

USDA HARDINESS ZONE	SUNSET HARDINESS ZONE	SIZE
9-10	13, 15-24	Variable with variety; 30"-6'
9-10	15-17, 23-24	6'
4	1-11, 14-17	Dwarf types 2'; species 6'+
10	16-24	6'-15'
9	8-9, 12-24	6'-15'
8	4-9, 14-26	Variable; 3'-10'
10	13, 17, 19-24	6'-8'
7	7-9, 12-24	4'-6'
7	7-9, 12-24	4'-6'
2	1-9, 14-24	5'-8'
6	2-24	Procumbent; 2' tall by 8' wide
5	3-6, 14-17	2'-5'
4	2-9, 14-17	1'-2'
4	2-9, 14-21	6'-20'
8	4-9, 14-17, 20-24	5'-10'
4-8	1-9, 14-20	8'-10'
3	1-9, 14-16	4'-8'
7-9	5-20	2'
7-9	5-20	2'
5	3-9, 14-17	3'
8	7-9, 12-16, 18-23	2'-6'
10	9, 12-13, 15-16, 19-24	4'- 8'
5	1-21	4'-8'
8	2-24	3'-6'
5	1-22	4'-6'
7	8-9, 14-16, 18-21	3'-8'
4	1-7, 16-17	8'-20'
9-10	14-24	1'-15'
7	6-14, 14-24	3'-10'
7	6-9, 14-24	4'-10'
9-10	9-13, 16-24	6'-15'
8	8-24	5'-8'
9-10	8-9, 12-24	4'-10'
7	5-24	18"-8'
7-8	8-16, 18-23	3'-10'
7	4-9, 14-21	4'-8'
7	3-10, 14-24	3'-5'
7	4-24	4'-8'
5	1-9, 14-17	5'-8'
8	8-24	4'-15'
7	4-9, 14-24	4'-15'
8	8-10, 12-24	3'-5'
6	4-24	1'-6'
3	1-7, 14-17	6'-10'
7	4-9, 14-22	2'-4'
4	1-9, 14-24	4'-6'
5	1-11, 14-17	4'-6'

pots, plants can be moved in out of the cold, and good drainage is simply a matter of using the right soil mix.

Growing shrubs in containers does present a few peculiar challenges, but isn't really much different from growing shrubs in the ground. Sun and shade requirements remain the same, and regular fertilizing is important to maintain good growth and leaf color. Of course, watering is the most critical aspect of maintenance. One hot afternoon in bone-dry soil can be the death of many potted plants. Containerized shrubs should be thoroughly soaked and then the soil should be allowed to become dry to the touch before more water is added.

Shrubs need repotting occasionally; either into larger pots if you want the plant to grow, or into the same pot time after time, following root and top pruning. This not only keeps the specimen from growing too large but also enables you to freshen up the soil by replacing at least a part of it. After repotting, shrubs respond with fresh, vigorous root and top growth; shrubs that are pot-bound or root-bound at first languish and ultimately decline.

Some plants tolerate container growing better than others (see the chart on the previous pages). Many fast-growing plants are poor candidates for containers because they need almost constant repotting. On the other hand, relatively slow-growing plants can make excellent container subjects.

There are two things to avoid with container-grown shrubs. First, whenever repotting, avoid the often disastrous practice of removing a plant by pulling it out of the pot by the stems or trunk. Always invert the pot (if possible) to let gravity help remove the soil mass, or lay the plant on its side, and gently coax the root ball out of the pot. Second, don't use pots without drainage holes; wet feet can be murder on your shrubs. If necessary, double-pot shrubs directly in a container with drainage, and then place this pot into a larger, decorative container without holes to catch the runoff.

From left to right: a gold-leaved cultivar of Japanese barberry, Harry Lauder's walking stick and camellia.

TEN TIPS FOR PROPER PRUNING

BY TED KIPPING

PRUNING CAN BE FUN with some forethought and basic knowledge, sharp tools and a little self-confidence. Remember that shrubs are living things that deserve our respect and that pruning is sculpting with life force.

Why bother pruning? Two reasons. Ideally, we should prune to remove damaged or diseased branches; to make a shrub more beautiful by editing or directing growth; to shape shrubs into an effective screen or thin them to open up a view; and to enhance the quality or quantity of flowers and fruits or, conversely, to inhibit them. In reality, though, about 90 percent of the pruning done by homeowners is undertaken because there has been a misguided choice of plant material for the particular location. Either we ourselves made the mistake or we inherited somebody else's mistake and are forced to do something about it.

1. KNOW BEFORE YOU GROW.

And that brings me to my first tip. Most pruning problems could be avoided by planting the correct plant in the correct place in the first place. Consider the national obsession with so-called foundation plantings. Homeowners want immediate results, so they plant decent-sized shrubs that quickly grow to colossal proportions under the overhang of the roof. The shrubs soon obscure the house, begin scraping the paint off the siding and invite burglars. Ultimately, they begin uprooting the foundation (hence, I'm convinced, the term foundation plants). Or, in another common practice, a gate or path gets "framed" with a couple of similarly rampant growers, and the hapless homeowners spend the rest of their lives trying to keep the space gouged out. Such savage pruning invariably distorts the shrub's shape. In such cases, the most humane course of action for all concerned is to replace the overly large plant with a specimen that naturally fits the space.

Shrubs such as Japanese kerria bloom on the previous season's shoots. These plants should be pruned back to vigorous new growth as soon as the flowers fade. At planting time, far left, remove damaged or weak stems and tip back main shoots to a strong pair of buds.

2. KNOW BEFORE YOU GO.

Size isn't the only consideration. Every shrub not only attains a certain size but also has its own inherent architecture or form. One may be bolt upright, another low and mounded and still another gracefully weeping. Don't try to force-prune a shrub into a shape contrary to its natural growing habit; although you may temporarily achieve your goal, keeping it that way will be a never-ending task and the plant will never achieve its full beauty. Before cutting a single stem ask yourself: Why am I growing this? What do I want it to accomplish? How can I help this shrub do what it wants to do?

Familiarize yourself not only with how your species grows but also, if it's a flowering shrub, when it blooms. This is crucial because if you prune at the proper time, you can enhance flower production; but if you prune at the wrong time, you may wind up with no flowers until the following year (more on this in a minute).

If the specimen is large enough, don't be afraid to poke your head inside the foliage to get a good look at the plant's architecture before proceeding.

3. SPRITZ BEFORE YOU SNIP.

Give your plant a good hosing down before you prune to get all the dust off. It's amazing how many particulates can accumulate on one shrub. You don't have to choke on this stuff.

4. MASTER THE FOUR D'S.

Elementary school students need to learn the three R's. Pruners must master the four D's regarding what to prune: the *D*ead, the *D*amaged, the *D*iseased and the

Butterfly bush and other shrubs that bloom on the current season's wood should be pruned way back in early spring, before new growth begins. At planting time, near right, remove weak or damaged branches and tip back main shoots.

Deranged. The first three are obvious. The fourth merits some additional discussion.

Deranged branches are those that go against the general rhythm and architecture of the plant — that violate its gestalt, so to speak — or work counter to its basic strength or productivity. For example, if you have a weeping plant you may want to remove a branch that's growing in an upsweeping fashion.

The four D's are removed by thinning. Thinning makes your shrubs look better, and also enhances their health by allowing for better air flow, better light penetration (and therefore photosynthesis) and better access for the good bugs that eat the bad bugs that pester the plants. This means you'll have to spray less often, if at all. Recently I was thinning a specimen with what at first glance looked like one-inch branches. When I started pruning, I realized that the branches were really only half an inch wide; the other half consisted of a solid crust of scale insects. Where I thinned, hornets immediately moved in and began scarfing up the pests. Six weeks later, the scale were gone.

Thinning can also add a bit of mystery to your garden by creating a lacy effect that affords a "peekaboo" view through a shrub or shrubs to give a hint of what lies beyond. As always, you want to make sure that you work with the rhythm of the plants, expressing their innate architecture. The peekaboo technique is useful if you're, say, breaking up a landscape into separate garden "rooms," to provide an enticing view that will draw visitors into the next space, or if you're designing a winding path and need a teasing glimpse of what lies beyond to encourage people to continue to explore the landscape.

5. OFF WITH THE DEAD WOOD FIRST.

If you don't know where to start, it's always safest to take out all the dead wood first. You can't go wrong. Even if you later decide to remove the branch you cleaned up, you haven't made any mistakes while you've been getting acquainted with the shrub.

6. TIP BEFORE YOU STRIP.

If you need to control the size of a shrub to some extent, you should tip back the branches before you do any thinning (with the exception of dead wood). Only then should you reach in to feather out overly dense limbs and remove crossing and competing branches. Otherwise, you may get carried away and end up stripping out a lot more foliage than you intended.

7. TO GROW OR NOT TO GROW?

Shaping and thinning can either retard or accelerate growth. The later in the season that you tip back, the more of a retarding effect the shaping will have. On the other hand, when you thin early in the season, you focus the plant's resources on a smaller number of growing tips, and so they grow more vigorously.

8. TIPS ON TIPPING BACK.

When choosing where to shorten or tip back a branch, keep in mind that upward-pointing buds will grow rapidly and upwards, whereas downward-pointing ones will grow relatively slowly. So, prune back to a downward-pointing bud or leaf if you're trying to make the shrub compact, and a vertical bud if you want it to grow taller. If you're dealing with a shrub with buds that come in pairs, choose a pair that are left and right, not top and bottom.

9. TO BLOOM OR NOT TO BLOOM?

Skillful pruning can either enhance bloom or inhibit it. Why would anyone want to keep a shrub from blooming? Some shrubs are grown for their foliage — for example, goldflame spirea. The foliage of this plant has a warm golden glow. However, this heart-warming glow is totally eclipsed by the plant's bone-chilling magenta flowers. Thus, many people cut the flower shoots off. Another example: The woody groundcover *Helichrysum* 'Moe's Gold' has a splendid mounding, silvery form, but also metallic-yellow flowers that destroy the effect of the silver. Therefore, many gardeners shear off the blossoms. Shearing buds off a shrub too close to a patio or path will also inhibit messy fruit drop.

Pruning shrubs that flower on the current year's wood. Most of the

Shrubs such as red-twig dog-wood, which are grown pri-marily for the decorative effect of young stems in win-ter, should be pruned hard in early spring to produce as many new shoots as possible. At planting time, near right, cut out all weak stems from the base and shorten remain-ing branches.

time, however, the goal is to encourage flowers, not get rid of them. And if you want to enhance the number or quality of blooms, then knowing when the buds form is critical. For instance, shrubs that flower on the current year's wood, such as oakleaf hydrangea, early-blooming buddleias, barberry, weigelas, blossoming spireas and shrub honeysuckles, should be dormant-pruned — that is to say, pruned in the early spring to promote vigorous new growth and increase the number of blooms. Early in the season is also a good time to cut off the new shoots, or candles, of coniferous shrubs. If you're trying to keep the plant com-pact, cut the candles off at the base. If you want to make the shrub denser, short-en the candle but be sure to cut where there are still some needles; if you cut by the stem, below the needles, you'll be left with an unsightly stub.

Pruning shrubs that bloom on last year's wood. The best time to prune shrubs that bloom on shoots produced in the previous growing season is after they have flowered. In other words, you're basically deadheading them. This annual pruning keeps the shrubs compact and shapely, but must be done imme-diately after flowering to give new wood time to develop and produce buds before winter. Examples of shrubs in this category are *Forsythia, Deutzia, Ker-ria, Philadelphus* and lilacs.

Stooling. A few shrubs should be cut back hard in early spring to obtain maximum effect from their decorative stems. This practice is often called "stool-ing," because the shrub is cut back to a stump low enough to sit on (like a stool). Growing plants for their colorful stems in the winter garden is becoming increasingly popular. The new growth of certain dogwoods, for example, is a striking red or gold. The old growth isn't nearly as showy. Consequently, just as new growth is about to set in, all of the existing branches are cut back to the base (you can cut back to one fat bud per shoot if you like, or leave a few longer shoots).

10. DON'T FLUSH CUT YOUR SHRUB DOWN THE DRAIN.

Last but not least is the matter of how to execute a proper cut. A bad cut is not only unsightly but also can lead to decay problems. Stubs are obviously sources of decay, but "flush" cuts, which remove the branch collar (the thicker area where the branch attaches to a primary branch or the trunk), also expose the plant to decay. A correct pruning cut removes the branch but retains the branch collar.

When tipping back, shorten the branches as close to the new terminal buds as you can without injuring the buds or weakening the point where they attach to the branch — remember, those buds are going to grow into new shoots.

A neglected shrub or one that has outgrown its space can often benefit from a drastic pruning. The lilac illustrated at left, for example, which has become bare at the base, is cut back hard sometime between late autumn and late winter. The following spring, near left, remove weak branches and those not growing upright.

The New Glamour Plants

The scores of spectacular shrubs that follow are listed in alphabetical order by botanical name; see the index for an alphabetical listing by common name. Individual listings include the shrub's native habitat and hardiness zone, growing and design tips and selected cultivars and related species. To find your hardiness zone, check the map on page 106; if you live in the West, consult the detailed maps in *Sunset Western Garden Book*, published by the editors of Sunset Books and *Sunset* magazine. For recommended shrubs for your region, see page 103.

Glossy Abelia

OUTSTANDING FEATURES: A graceful, arching, deciduous shrub with oval, glossy leaves and bronzy new growth. Pink tubular or bell-shaped flowers flushed with white appear at the ends of branches or among leaves from June through October.

NATIVE HABITAT
Hybrid

HARDINESS ZONE
USDA 5-9
Sunset 5-24

HABIT AND GARDEN USE: Grows to 8' tall and gracefully arches to 5' wide or more. An adaptable plant useful in mixed shrub borders, as space dividers and as visual barriers.

HOW TO GROW: Prefers full sun, acid, well-drained soils. To preserve open, arching form, selectively prune stems to ground in winter or early spring.

CULTIVARS AND RELATED SPECIES

'Edward Goucher' — Lower growing (3'-5' tall), with a more lacy appearance. Lilac-pink flowers with orange throats make a showy display.

A. chinensis — Upright grower 5'-7' tall with sweetly scented white flowers.

Abelia x *grandiflora* 'Sherwoodii', a dwarf cultivar

OUTSTANDING FEATURES: A wonderful, coarse-textured shrub with broad, maplelike leaves grown outdoors in warmer regions and indoors in colder climates. Its drooping, bell-shaped flowers in white, yellow, pink, lavender and red look like Chinese lanterns and bloom almost continuously.

HABIT AND GARDEN USE: Grows 8'-10' tall outdoors, with an equal arching spread. Its growth is rapid and often rangy, but can be attractively controlled by pinching branch tips. Can be trained as an informal espalier against a wall or as a standard in a container.

HOW TO GROW: Prefers moist, partial shade; does not tolerate dry, windy conditions. Pinch often to encourage denser foliage and good form. Prone to whitefly and scale insects, especially when grown indoors, but these can be controlled with horticultural oil and insecticidal soap sprays.

Flowering Maple

NATIVE HABITAT
South America

HARDINESS ZONE
USDA 9-10
Sunset 8-9, 12-24

Abutilon x *hybridum*

The bell-shaped flowers resemble Chinese lanterns.

Bottlebrush Buckeye

OUTSTANDING FEATURES: Among the finest of our native American shrubs for spectacular flowering and foliage effect. Valued for its showy, 8"-12" panicles of white flowers in early summer. Summer foliage is dark green and, unlike other buckeyes, is pest and disease free. In fall, the leaves turn bright yellow.

NATIVE HABITAT
South Carolina to Alabama and Florida

HARDINESS ZONE
USDA 4-8
Sunset 1-10, 12, 14-17

HABIT AND GARDEN USE: A wide-spreading, suckering, multi-stemmed shrub that colonizes to form a large, rounded outline 8'-12' in height with an equal or greater spread. Excellent for massing, shrub borders or as a specimen. Unsurpassed for summer flowering and fall color.

HOW TO GROW: Prefers moist, well-drained soils in full sun to partial shade, although it tolerates poorer soils and full shade without apparent reduction in growth or flowering. Best transplanted balled and burlapped or from a container. No serious pest or disease problems.

CULTIVARS AND RELATED SPECIES

A.p. serotina — A naturally occurring variety of the species from Alabama that flowers 2 to 3 weeks later.

'Rogers' — A cultivar that produces 18"-30" panicles and flowers later than both the species and variety *serotina*.

Aesculus parviflora, with "bottlebrush" blooms

OUTSTANDING FEATURES: A remarkably attractive shrub grown for its round, reddish yellow fruits that are strawberry-like in appearance, but not taste. Drooping clusters of white, urn-shaped flowers precede the fruits. Bark is dark reddish brown and shreds with age; leaves are dark green with red petioles.

Strawberry Tree

HABIT AND GARDEN USE: The best forms are the cultivars listed below, which grow into dense shrubs 5'-12' tall at maturity with equal spreads. Easily pruned or sculpted into more picturesque, open-branched forms. Best planted in lawns, mixed borders and raised planters.

NATIVE HABITAT
Southern Europe

HARDINESS ZONE
USDA 8-9
Sunset 4-24

HOW TO GROW: Easy to grow in full sun. Adaptable to a wide range of soils when planted outdoors in warmer regions. Requires little water once established, but tolerates lots of water in well-drained soils. No serious pests or diseases.

CULTIVARS AND RELATED SPECIES
'Compacta' — Smaller, shrubby form growing to 8'-15' tall.
'Elfin King' — Picturesque, contorted dwarf form 5'-8' tall, which flowers and fruits continuously. Excellent container plant.

Urn-shaped flowers

Arbutus unedo, with strawberry-like fruits

Red Chokeberry

OUTSTANDING FEATURES: A widely adaptable shrub native to a large portion of the U.S. Grown for outstanding foliage and fruit as well as its tolerance of a wide range of soils and exposures. Bright red fruits are borne in profusion along the branches in late summer and persist well into winter. Fall color is bright red-purple and lasts for several weeks.

NATIVE HABITAT
Massachusetts to Florida, west to Minnesota, Ohio, Arizona and Texas

HARDINESS ZONE
USDA 4-9
Sunset 1-7

HABIT AND GARDEN USE: Distinctly upright, taller than wide; branches generally arch under the weight of the fruit. Size is 6'-8' in height with a spread of 3'-5'. Can form large colonies if allowed to sucker. Excellent for massing or used in the mixed border where perennials and other shorter shrubs will help to cover the bare lower stems. Among the finest shrubs for fall foliage and showy fruit.

HOW TO GROW: Widely adaptable to soil types; transplants easily bare root or from containers. Full sun to partial shade, although fall color and fruiting are enhanced in full sun. Periodically, older stems should be pruned to the ground to encourage rejuvenation. No serious pests or diseases.

CULTIVARS AND RELATED SPECIES

'Brilliantissima' — This cultivar has lustrous, dark green leaves that become brilliant red in the fall. Similar in other respects to the species.

A. melanocarpa, Black Chokeberry — Similar to red chokeberry in habit and leaf color; fruits are blackish purple when ripe.

Aronia arbutifolia

The bright red fruits persist well into winter.

OUTSTANDING FEATURES: Despite its spiny branches, a graceful shrub if not sheared into contrived forms. Dense foliage; the small, roundish, deep green leaves turn yellow, orange and red before they drop in autumn. Bead-like, bright red berries are effective in the winter garden.

HABIT AND GARDEN USE: Slender, arching shrub usually reaching 4'-6' tall with equal spread. Excellent for hedges, barrier plantings, as a single specimen or mixed in borders. Cultivars with reddish or purplish foliage are available.

HOW TO GROW: This easy-care shrub tolerates climate and soil extremes. Provide sun or light shade and average water. No serious pests or diseases.

CULTIVARS AND RELATED SPECIES

'Atropurpurea' — Reddish to purplish foliage in sun; 3'-6' tall by 4'-8' wide.

'Crimson Pygmy' — Popular miniature form less than 1-1/2' tall and 2-1/2' wide; bronzy, blood-red leaves in full sun.

'Rose Glow' — Rose-pink leaves mottled with deeper red-purple splotches; 5'-6' tall.

Japanese Barberry

NATIVE HABITAT
Japan

HARDINESS ZONE
USDA 4-8
Sunset 1-24

'Crimson Pygmy', a miniature form

Thorny *Berberis thunbergii* in fruit

Angel's Trumpet

NATIVE HABITAT
Ecuador

HARDINESS ZONE
USDA 10
Sunset 16-24

Brugmansia versicolor 'Frosty Pink'

OUTSTANDING FEATURES: A big, bold shrub with large, show-stopping, tubular white or peach-colored flowers, flared at the mouth — hence the common name angel's trumpet. Flowers are fragrant, especially at night. Large, tropical-looking leaves 8"-12" long cover this quick-grower.

HABIT AND GARDEN USE: An upright, sparsely branched, rounded shrub growing to 15' tall. A dominating form in the garden that should be carefully sited; best used as a specimen plant in the ground or containers.

HOW TO GROW: Plant in sun or partial shade in wind-sheltered locations. Requires ample moisture during the growing season. Expect periodic frost damage and unattractive winter appearance in regions where it is borderline hardy. Plants in tubs can be wintered indoors with very little light and water. Whiteflies and spider mites can be troublesome.

CULTIVARS AND RELATED SPECIES
'Charles Grimaldi' — Pale, orange-yellow blooms.
'Frosty Pink' — Cream-colored trumpets, deepening to pink with age.

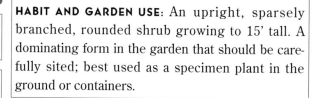

'Charles Grimaldi'

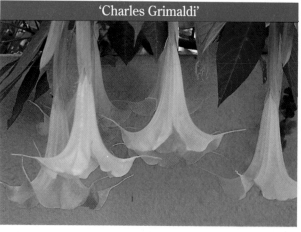

OUTSTANDING FEATURES: A summer bloomer with dense, arching, spiky, 6"-12" clusters of lilac-colored, mildly fragrant flowers at the ends of the branches. A magnet for butterflies in the garden. Dark green leaves, 4"-12" long, are white and felted underneath.

HABIT AND GARDEN USE: Fast, rank growth each spring, from 3'-10' tall, depending on cultivar. Deciduous in most regions; semi-evergreen in warmer zones. Use in mixed borders and habitat gardens for summer sparkle and color.

HOW TO GROW: Requires good drainage and enough water to maintain growth — little else. Whether deciduous or semi-evergreen (in mild winter areas), cut plants back to within a few inches of the ground in late winter before new growth for best appearance. In hot, dry areas may be susceptible to red spider mites.

CULTIVARS AND RELATED SPECIES
'Black Knight' — Dark purple flower clusters.
'Petite Plum' — Reddish purple flowers with an orange eye on compact, many-branched shrub.
B. alternifolia, Fountain Butterfly Bush — Hardy species and the first to flower in the spring, with lilac-purple clusters on previous year's growth. Arching form with long, pendulous shoots reminiscent of a small weeping willow.

Common Butterfly Bush

NATIVE HABITAT
China

HARDINESS ZONE
USDA 5-9
Sunset 1-24

'Border Beauty'

Buddleia davidii 'Ile de France'

Red Bird-of-Paradise Shrub

OUTSTANDING FEATURES: A handsome flowering, deciduous shrub popular in desert and warm inland gardens of the Southwest. Finely divided leaves and an open branching habit. Produces spectacular orange-yellow flowers at branch tips during spring and summer.

NATIVE HABITAT
Mexico

HARDINESS ZONE
USDA 9-10
Sunset 12-16,
18-23

HABIT AND GARDEN USE: Mounding form 6'-10' high with an equal spread. Best used as a colorful accent shrub in a courtyard or as a screen and background plant to enclose a garden.

HOW TO GROW: Prefers well-drained, slightly acid soils and periodic deep watering. Requires full sun and responds well to summer heat; does not thrive in cool, humid environments.

CULTIVARS AND RELATED SPECIES
C. gilliesii, Bird-of-Paradise — Large, terminal clusters of yellow flowers with red stamens; 6'-10' tall.

Caesalpinia pulcherrima in summer, with its vibrant, orange-yellow flowers

OUTSTANDING FEATURES: A show-stopping shrub with unusual color in October when the long, slender branches that arch and sweep the ground are loaded with small, 1/8"-diameter, lilac-violet fruits. Small, pinkish lavender flower clusters borne on stalks above the foliage precede the fruits from June through August.

Purple Beautyberry

HABIT AND GARDEN USE: Grows 3'-4' high with a 4'-5' spread. Allow plenty of room for plant to drape, or plant in masses of 3-5 for a spectacular effect. A good plant in mixed borders or alone in a sea of groundcover, such as *Ajuga reptans* 'Burgundy Glow'.

NATIVE HABITAT
China, Japan

HARDINESS ZONE
USDA 5-8
Sunset 1-6

HOW TO GROW: Plant in full sun in average garden soil. Best treated as a herbaceous perennial by cutting to the ground each year and encouraging new growth. No serious pests or diseases.

CULTIVARS AND RELATED SPECIES
C.d. albifructus — White-fruited form.
C. americana, American Beautyberry — U.S. native with violet-magenta fruits produced in profusion. Good shrub for naturalizing or massing.

The striking lilac fruits of *Callicarpa dichotoma*

Carolina Allspice

OUTSTANDING FEATURES: Unusual reddish brown flowers borne singly in the leaf axils from May into June and July in Brooklyn. Flowers are up to 2" across, with a pleasing fruity fragrance that permeates the surrounding area. Dark green foliage can become golden yellow in fall.

NATIVE HABITAT
Virginia to Florida

HARDINESS ZONE
USDA 4-9
Sunset 1-9, 14-22

HABIT AND GARDEN USE: An adaptable U.S. native for use in massing, the mixed border or as a single specimen. Especially nice when located near a patio or window, where the fragrance can be enjoyed. Habit is dense and rounded, 6'-8' in height with an equal or greater spread. Can be kept smaller with minimal pruning.

HOW TO GROW: Transplants easily from containers or balled and burlapped. Prefers moist, well-drained soils but tolerates a wide range of soil types and full sun to partial shade. Plants tend to be more compact in sun. Pruning, when needed, should be done after flowering. No serious pest or disease problems.

CULTIVARS AND RELATED SPECIES

'Athens' — A highly fragrant yellow-flowered form thought to have originated in Athens, Georgia.

'Edith Wilder' — A red-flowered form selected by the Scott Arboretum of Swarthmore College for its intensely wine-scented flowers.

C. occidentalis, California Sweetshrub — Similar to *C. floridus* except larger and less fragrant; native to California.

The flowers of *Calycanthus floridus* have a pleasing fruity fragrance.

OUTSTANDING FEATURES: A lustrous, broadleaved evergreen with showy, 3"-5" diameter flowers in white, pink, rose, red and combinations thereof. Flowers vary from single to double and from peony to anemone to rose forms. Generally blooms from November through April, depending on climate zone.

Japanese Camellia

HABIT AND GARDEN USE: Generally upright and pyramidal, 6'-12' tall, in a rather stiff and formal way. Excellent planted in mixed borders and as focal points in protected courtyards or espaliered against walls.

NATIVE HABITAT
China, Japan

HARDINESS ZONE
USDA 7-9
Sunset 4-9, 12, 14-24

HOW TO GROW: Camellias prefer, moist, acid, well-drained soils rich in organic matter. Plant in partial shade for best flowering. Prune after flowering. Cold weather and freezes turn flowers mushy brown, cause dieback and can kill plants. Pests and diseases can be controlled by planting this shrub in a suitable site.

A cultivar with semi-double blooms

CULTIVARS AND RELATED SPECIES
'Debutante' — Light pink, peony form.
'Kramer's Supreme' — Clear red, full peony form.
'Magnoliiflora' — Light pink, semi-double flowers.
'Purity' — White, rose-like flowers.
C. sasanqua — More diminutive, refined shrub, 6'-10' tall, with smaller leaves and flowers.

A white, single-flowered form

Bluebeard, Blue-spirea

OUTSTANDING FEATURES: Unsurpassed for its intensely blue, late-season flowers. Flower clusters appear in late summer and are effective for several weeks; color ranges from blues to purples, depending on the cultivar.

NATIVE HABITAT
Hybrid

HARDINESS ZONE
USDA 6-9
Sunset 1-7, 14-17

HABIT AND GARDEN USE: Bluebeard is a mounded, twiggy shrub best cut back annually, like an herbaceous perennial. The plant forms a rounded mound up to 4' in height, depending on the cultivar. This is an excellent choice for mixed borders and around pools, combined with grasses and other late-summer perennials. Bluebeard is also excellent for cut flowers.

HOW TO GROW: Best in full sun and dry soils. Cut to the ground annually in spring. In colder areas, plants may die to the ground in winter, but will flower by late summer. No serious pests and diseases.

CULTIVARS AND RELATED SPECIES
'Blue Mist' — Powder-blue flowers.
'Dark Knight' — Deep blue-purple flowers.
'Longwood Blue' — Bluish violet flowers and gray-green foliage.

Caryopteris x *clandonenis,* unsurpassed for its intensely blue flowers

OUTSTANDING FEATURES: One of the hardiest ever-green *Ceanothus* with showy, light to dark blue, 3", spikelike flower clusters in March and April. Glossy leaves up to 2" long are attractive year-round.

HABIT AND GARDEN USE: A large, mounded shrub from 6'-21' tall, often attaining an equal spread. Best planted in masses for background effect, on dry slopes and banks or as single specimens isolated from other plants with high water requirements. Also striking as an espalier against a fence.

HOW TO GROW: A short-lived plant in a garden setting; 5-10 years is average. Can easily succumb to root rot in heavy, water-retentive soils or gardens too frequently irrigated. Plant beyond the reach of sprinklers or in dry zones of the garden with other drought-tolerant plants. Powdery mildew can also be a problem. No serious insect pests.

CULTIVARS AND RELATED SPECIES
'Julia Phelps' — Rich, dark indigo blue; one of the best bloomers.
C. americanus, New Jersey Tea — Native to the eastern U.S. Hardiest of the *Ceanothus*; USDA zones 4 to 8. White flower clusters June to July.

California
Lilac

NATIVE HABITAT
California to Oregon

HARDINESS ZONE
USDA 8-9
Sunset 4-7, 14-24

'Julia Phelps'

Ceanothus thyrsiflorus in spring, with flowers

Flowering Quince

OUTSTANDING FEATURES: Highly valued for the effect of the flowers on bare branches as early as January to March in the South and West and April farther north. Flower color ranges widely, from orange, reddish orange, scarlet and carmine to pink to white. When in bloom it is highly praised; as a foliage plant it is hardly noticed.

NATIVE HABITAT
China

HARDINESS ZONE
USDA 4-8
Sunset 1-21

Multicolored 'Toyo-Nishiki'

HABIT AND GARDEN USE: A rounded shrub with a tangled mass of spiny branches. Some forms are more upright; others, rambling. Plant in masses as a barrier hedge or use as accent plants in mixed borders.

HOW TO GROW: Adaptable to many soil types and moisture levels. Plant in full sun and eliminate older branches or cut back the shrub each year for more spectacular flowering. Leaf spot can almost defoliate plants after a wet spring.

CULTIVARS AND RELATED SPECIES
'Cameo' — Double, fluffy apricot-pink flowers.
'Texas Scarlet' — Bright red flowers on compact, spreading plant.
C. x *superba* — Hybrid, with good low-growing cultivars.

Espaliering *Chaenomeles speciosa* is a way to show the shrub to best effect.

OUTSTANDING FEATURES: A winter bloomer with fragrance to boot! Pale yellow flowers on leafless stems with a spicy aroma from late winter to early spring, depending on the region of the country. Lustrous, dark green leaves 3"-6" long are attractive through the growing season and offer yellow-green hues in the fall.

HABIT AND GARDEN USE: Tall and open in form, it grows 10'-15' tall and 6'-8' wide. Be sure to plant this shrub where you can enjoy its winter fragrance — near an entrance or bedroom window, for example, or in a courtyard where its appealing aroma is less apt to waft away.

HOW TO GROW: Easy to grow in full sun or partial shade. Adaptable to various soils, but requires good drainage. Prune out old stems after they flower or remove excess stems and shape as a small multi-stemmed tree. No serious pests or diseases.

Fragrant Wintersweet

NATIVE HABITAT
China

HARDINESS ZONE
USDA 7-9
Sunset 4-7, 8-9,
14-17

The flowers have a spicy aroma.

Chimonanthus praecox blooms in winter.

Mexican orange

OUTSTANDING FEATURES: Fragrant white flower clusters, somewhat like small orange blossoms, continuously blooming from early spring into April in warmer climates, later in borderline regions. Lustrous evergreen leaves are borne at the ends of branches and divided into fans of 3 leaflets for a dense, layered look.

NATIVE HABITAT
Mexico

HARDINESS ZONE
USDA 7-9
Sunset 7-9, 12-17

The flowers are fragrant.

HABIT AND GARDEN USE: A rounded, fast grower 6'-8' high with an equal spread. In warm regions it is attractive massed as an informal hedge lining paths and entranceways or planted as a specimen in a courtyard, where fragrance will be concentrated. Adventuresome gardeners in regions where winter temperatures drop below 10°-15° F can grow this shrub in containers.

HOW TO GROW: Grows in full sun to partial shade. Somewhat touchy about soil conditions — especially alkaline soils high in salts. Subject to root and crown rot in poorly drained soils. Mites and other sucking insects can be troublesome.

CULTIVARS AND RELATED SPECIES
'Sundance' — Golden foliage, especially on new growth.

Choisya ternata has handsome flowers and foliage.

OUTSTANDING FEATURES: Cheery, sun-loving, reddish purple, 3"-wide flowers with red spots at the base of each petal during spring months in warmer regions. Leaves are dark green above, gray and hairy underneath, and on warm days emit an aroma evocative of the Mediterranean region.

HABIT AND GARDEN USE: A compact shrub growing to 4' tall with an equal spread. Fast growth, drought tolerance and fire retardance make this a versatile plant. Highly recommended in areas where cool winds and salt spray are limiting factors. Use as a bank cover, low divider or in dry mixed borders.

HOW TO GROW: Demands well-drained soil, especially if watered frequently, and likes full sun. Cut out a few old stems each season and tip-prune to encourage thick growth. Plants are prone to fungal diseases and root rot when grown in high humidity.

CULTIVARS AND RELATED SPECIES

C. hybridus, White Rockrose — White flowers with yellow centers; crinkly, 2"-long, gray-green leaves. Spreads 2'-5' high and wide.

Orchid Rockrose

NATIVE HABITAT
Hybrid

HARDINESS ZONE
USDA 8-9
Sunset 16-17, 23-24

Cistus x *purpureus*

The three-inch-wide, poppy-like flowers appear in spring.

Summer-sweet

OUTSTANDING FEATURES: A distinctive, deciduous shrub noted for its spicy sweet summertime (July and August) blooms on branch tips that produce several 4"-6"-long spires of tiny, gleaming white flowers. Attractive dark green leaves 2"-4" long with toothed edges appear very late, in mid-May. Pale yellow to golden fall color.

NATIVE HABITAT
Eastern United States

HARDINESS ZONE
USDA 3-9
Sunset 2-6

HABIT AND GARDEN USE: Grows to 10' tall with thin but strong vertical branches. Spreads slowly by suckers into broad, dense clumps. A great shrub in borders, natural shade gardens and wet soils.

HOW TO GROW: Likes moist, acid organic soils. Tolerates shade or full sun; for best results, grow it in partial shade where summers are hot. Grows naturally in wet areas and withstands coastal salt spray.

CULTIVARS AND RELATED SPECIES
'Pink Spires' — Deep pink buds open to soft pink flowers.
'Hummingbird' — Dwarf cultivar that grows 3'-4' tall with an equal spread.

The blooms are spicy-sweet.

Clethra alnifolia, native to the eastern U.S.

OUTSTANDING FEATURES: A dogwood with a good show of reddish purple fall leaves and bright red winter twigs. Extremely eye-catching in the winter garden against a backdrop of snow. Flat-topped, dull white flower clusters appear throughout the summer but are relatively unremarkable.

HABIT AND GARDEN USE: Grows rapidly to a big, multi-stemmed thicket 7'-9' tall by 10' wide. Spreads freely by underground stems. Use this adaptable U.S. native as a space filler in moist soil, massed along property lines, planted on banks and slopes for soil stabilization or in mixed borders.

HOW TO GROW: Highly adaptable to a wide range of soil types, although it does best in moist locations. Tolerates both sun and shade. To keep it in bounds, cut off roots and stems that have strayed too far with a sharp spade.

CULTIVARS AND RELATED SPECIES
'Cardinal' — Cultivar originating in Minnesota, with bright, cherry-red stems.
'Flaviramea' — Yellow stems.
'Silver and Gold' — Yellow stems with creamy variegated leaves.

Red-twig Dogwood

NATIVE HABITAT
Eastern North America,
California to Alaska

HARDINESS ZONE
USDA 2-8
Sunset 1-9, 14-21

Cornus stolonifera, with red stems

'Flaviramea', yellow-twig dogwood

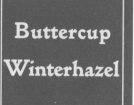

Buttercup Winterhazel

OUTSTANDING FEATURES: A delicate, fine-textured deciduous shrub grown for its fragrant primrose-yellow flowers, which appear in late March and early April in Brooklyn.

HABIT AND GARDEN USE: Vase-shaped, 4'-5' tall with an equal spread. Combines well with broadleaved evergreens and other early spring-flowering shrubs. One exquisite combination originated at Winterthur, the Wilmington, Delaware garden of the late Henry Francis du Pont, where the pale yellow flowers of the buttercup winterhazel appear with the soft rosy-purple flowers of *Rhododendron mucronulatum*, the Korean rhododendron.

NATIVE HABITAT
Japan and Taiwan

HARDINESS ZONE
USDA 6-8
Sunset 4-7, 15-17

HOW TO GROW: Needs of this plant are similar to those of rhododendrons; prefers moist soil in partial shade. Does poorly in soils with a high pH. Requires protection from hot sun and drying winds. No serious pest or disease problems.

CULTIVARS AND RELATED SPECIES

C. spicata, Spike Winterhazel — Similar to the buttercup winterhazel except larger. 4'-6' tall, with a spread of 8'-12'. Flower color and bloom time are essentially the same.

The primrose-yellow flowers of *Corylopsis pauciflora* are fragrant.

OUTSTANDING FEATURES: Grown for the unusual twisted stems and leaves which, along with the male catkins, combine to give quite a remarkable winter effect. Catkins begin flowering in mid to late March and reach 1-1/2"-3" in length when fully open. Branches can be cut at any time during the winter and brought indoors for forcing.

Harry Lauder's Walking Stick

HABIT AND GARDEN USE: Habit is generally quite rounded, 8'-10' tall with an equal spread. Plants are usually multistemmed and branched rather low to the ground, which limits underplanting. Best used as a specimen, in foundation plantings or combined with other plants for winter interest.

NATIVE HABITAT
Hybrid

HARDINESS ZONE
USDA 4- 8
Sunset 1-9, 14-20

Corylus avellana 'Contorta' in early spring

HOW TO GROW: Transplant Harry Lauder's walking stick either balled and burlapped or from a container. This shrub prefers moist, well-drained soil in full sun to partial shade, although it tends to be adaptable. Most plants available commercially are grafted, and thus constant attention must be given to removing the suckers, which invariably will arise from the base; the suckers will not have the prized, contorted form. This shrub has no serious pest or disease problems.

Smokebush

NATIVE HABITAT
Southern Europe to China

HARDINESS ZONE
USDA 4-8
Sunset 1-3, 10-11

OUTSTANDING FEATURES: Unusual multistemmed shrub with loose clusters of fading flowers clothed with fuzzy, purple hairs that look like puffs of lavender smoke from June to August. The roundish leaves are blue-green and turn orange-red in fall.

HABIT AND GARDEN USE: Broad, loose and open form, often wider than tall (10'-12'). A great accent or focal point in mixed borders, especially the purple-leaved forms; can also hold its own as a single specimen.

HOW TO GROW: Adapted to a wide range of soil types and pH ranges. Plant in well-drained, loamy soil and full sun for best performance. No serious pest or disease problems.

CULTIVARS AND RELATED SPECIES

'Royal Purple' — The darkest purple-leaved form whose color does not fade in summer; good red-purple fall color, too.

'Velvet Cloak' — Handsome, dark purple foliage with some fading in summer; excellent reddish purple in autumn.

Cotinus coggygria has smoke-like puffs of fading flowers from June to August.

OUTSTANDING FEATURES: Dark, glossy green summer foliage that turns shades of red and purple in the fall combined with an outstanding fruit display make this an excellent choice for low-maintenance mass plantings. Valued for its overall durability and tolerance of a wide range of soil types and exposures.

HABIT AND GARDEN USE: Low, wide-spreading shrub with arching branches that display a herringbone pattern. Height can reach 3' with a spread to 3'-6'. Flowers are pinkish white and appear in late spring, followed by bright red fruits that ripen in late summer and can persist for several months. Excellent for massing, banks, foundation plantings and the mixed border. Combines well with broadleaved evergreens.

HOW TO GROW: Best transplanted from a container. Widely adaptable to soil types and exposures. Periodically, older branches should be pruned out to rejuvenate the shrub. Spider mites can be troublesome in dry situations.

CULTIVARS AND RELATED SPECIES

C. dammeri, Bearberry Cotoneaster — Among the best evergreen groundcovers, particularly in the northern part of its hardiness range. Flowers, fruit and evergreen foliage combine to make this an outstanding groundcover.

C. salicifolius, Willowleaf Cotoneaster — A larger, evergreen species valued for its especially showy fruit display.

Cranberry Cotoneaster

NATIVE HABITAT
Western China

HARDINESS ZONE
USDA 4-7
Sunset 1-24

Cotoneaster apiculatus

The bright red fruits can last for months.

Burkwood Daphne

NATIVE HABITAT
Hybrid

HARDINESS ZONE
USDA 4-8
Sunset 1-24

'Somerset', a pink-flowered cultivar

OUTSTANDING FEATURES: Grown for the beautiful foliage (variegated on some cultivars) and fragrant white to pink flowers borne in clusters in May and June.

HABIT AND GARDEN USE: A choice, deciduous to semi-evergreen shrub, 3' in height with an equal spread. Leaves are dark green; plant habit is compact. An excellent plant for smaller gardens, the mixed border and containers. Should be located close by where it can be enjoyed throughout the season.

HOW TO GROW: Transplant daphnes from containers in early spring or early fall. Be careful about site selection because these plants resent being moved. Soil should be moist with near-neutral pH and excellent drainage. Light shade is preferable; if exposed to winter sun, plants should be protected with pine boughs or salt marsh hay. Prune daphnes as needed, immediately after flowering. The genus has a reputation for "up and dying" for no apparent reason. This is probably due to a combination of factors; for example, stress due to both less-than-perfect drainage and high temperatures. Most problems can be avoided with proper site selection.

CULTIVARS AND RELATED SPECIES

'Carol Mackie' — A beautifully variegated cultivar with dark green leaves edged in cream.

D. caucasica, Caucasian Daphne — Deciduous, 4'-5' tall with an equal spread. Deliciously fragrant white flowers are borne in clusters at the ends of the branches during April and May and sporadically throughout the growing season. One of the parents of *D.* x *burkwoodii*.

OUTSTANDING FEATURES: Grown primarily for its compact habit and incredible spring floral display. Pure white flowers 1/2"-3/4" across are borne in clusters along the stems in such profusion that they literally obscure the rest of the plant.

HABIT AND GARDEN USE: Slender arching branches form a rounded mound. Plants will reach 2'-4' in height with an equal spread at maturity. Flowering occurs in mid-May in Brooklyn and is effective for 10-14 days. For use in hedging and shrub and mixed borders or in front of taller shrubs.

HOW TO GROW: Slender deutzia transplants readily into most soils. This shrub does best in full sun; anything less will drastically limit flowering. Pruning, when needed, should be done immediately after flowering in the spring. No serious pest or disease problems.

CULTIVARS AND RELATED SPECIES
'Nikko' — A charming dwarf selection that grows 12"-15" high with a spread of 3'-4'. In addition to the white flowers produced in spring, this cultivar develops an attractive burgundy fall color that persists for several weeks. Excellent for edging, rockeries and foundation plantings.

Slender Deutzia

NATIVE HABITAT
Japan

HARDINESS ZONE
USDA Zones: 4-8
Sunset 1-11, 14-17

The flowers are bright white.

Deutzia gracilis has a compact habit and incredible spring floral display.

Thorny Elaeagnus

OUTSTANDING FEATURES: Among the latest of the shrubs to bloom in the fall. Evergreen foliage is dark, glossy green on the upper side and silvery on the bottom. Flowers are obscured by the foliage, but the sweet fragrance (reminiscent of gardenias) permeates the air. Flowering begins in October and continues for several weeks into November.

NATIVE HABITAT
Japan

HARDINESS ZONE
USDA 6-9
Sunset 4-24

HABIT AND GARDEN USE: Tends to be a rather unkempt-looking shrub if left unpruned, particularly in the more southern parts of its range. Overall habit is rounded, but long shoots produced later in the season contribute to its untidy appearance. Best used for hedging or screening or as a barrier.

The fall flowers are fragrant.

HOW TO GROW: Thorny eleagnus is easily transplanted. Adaptable to a wide range of soil types and exposures, although plants grown in full sun will be more compact. Regular pruning (particularly removal of the long shoots) is necessary to keep the plant in bounds. No serious pest or disease problems.

CULTIVARS AND RELATED SPECIES
'Fruitlandii' — One of the most widely available forms. Leaves are larger and more rounded than the species.
'Maculata' — Large leaves marked with a prominent yellow blotch in the center.
'Variegata' — Leaves edged in bright yellow.

Elaeagnus pungens is one of the latest-blooming shrubs.

Eleutherococcus (Acanthopanax) sieboldianus 'Variegatus'

OUTSTANDING FEATURES: Strikingly variegated foliage characterizes this fast-growing, deciduous shrub. Leaves are palmately compound with five to seven green leaflets edged with creamy white.

HABIT AND GARDEN USE: Plant habit is upright to rounded, eventually reaching 6'-8' in height with an equal spread. Easily kept in bounds with regular pruning. A remarkably durable shrub that can be used for hedging, massing or as a single specimen. A bright spot in any garden, especially in shade.

HOW TO GROW: Prefers moist soil in partial shade, but is very tolerant of a wide range of soil types, as well as exposures, from full sun to full shade. Also tolerates air pollution. Adapts well to urban conditions. Leaf spot is occasionally reported but should not be a serious problem.

Variegated Fiveleaf Aralia

NATIVE HABITAT
Species native to Japan

HARDINESS ZONE
USDA 4-8
Sunset 1-21

The leaves are edged in cream.

Eleutherococcus sieboldianus 'Variegatus'

Redvein Enkianthus

NATIVE HABITAT
Japan

HARDINESS ZONE
USDA 4-8
Sunset 2-9, 14-21

Enkianthus campanulatus

OUTSTANDING FEATURES: Delicate bell-shaped flowers borne in short clusters in May and June. Flowers are pale yellow or orange with thin red veins running through them. Fall color ranges from yellow to orange to red.

HABIT AND GARDEN USE: A wonderfully delicate shrub 6'-8' in height with an equal spread. Branching pattern is tiered, creating a layered effect on older plants. Combines well with broadleaved evergreens; best when planted by a terrace or other area where its subtle beauty can be seen close up.

HOW TO GROW: Like rhododendrons, this enkianthus requires moist, acid, well-drained soil in full sun to partial shade. Transplants easily from containers or balled and burlapped. No serious pests or diseases.

CULTIVARS AND RELATED SPECIES

'Albiflorus' — Flowers are pure white, with orange-red fall leaf color.

'Red Bells' — Flowers are tipped in pure red, which is unusual for the species. Upper portion of the flower is typical soft yellow with red veins.

E. perulatus, White Enkianthus — Similar to redvein enkianthus in size and habit; flowers are white and appear before the leaves, resulting in a more showy effect. Leaves turn crimson in fall.

The delicate, bell-shaped flowers have thin red veins.

OUTSTANDING FEATURES: Among the earliest shrubs to flower in spring. Valued for its small, urn-shaped flowers in shades of white, pink and rose, borne amidst the fine-textured, needle-like evergreen foliage.

HABIT AND GARDEN USE: Makes an excellent groundcover. Combines well with perennials and other shrubs. Its early bloom and evergreen foliage provide a long season of interest. Can be mixed with heathers for a similar appearance and a longer period of bloom.

HOW TO GROW: Plant spring heath from containers in early spring. This plant demands a sandy, moist, acid, well-drained soil in full sun. Protect it from heavy winds, particularly in winter. Cut it back immediately after flowering to maintain vigor. Heaths have a reputation for being prone to fungal problems, but these can be avoided with proper soil preparation and site selection.

CULTIVARS AND RELATED SPECIES

E. arborea, Tree Heath — Similar to *E. carnea* except in size (10'-20' in height with a smaller spread) and not as hardy. Cultivated primarily on the West Coast.

Calluna vulgaris, Scotch Heather — Heaths and heathers, although different genera, are similar and often grown together. This heather is like *E. Carnea* in overall habit. Flowers appear in summer. Cut back before flowering in early spring.

Spring Heath

NATIVE HABITAT
Europe, Asia Minor

HARDINESS ZONE
USDA 4-7
Sunset 2-10, 14-24

Very early spring blooms

Erica carnea has tiny, urn-shaped flowers and needle-like evergreen foliage.

Red Escallonia

NATIVE HABITAT
Chile

HARDINESS ZONE
USDA 8
Sunset 4-9, 14-17,
20-24

Blooms are cheery red .

OUTSTANDING FEATURES: A clean-looking, fast-growing evergreen shrub. Leaves are smooth, very glossy, dark green. Cheery, 1"-3" clusters of red or crimson flowers appear throughout summer and fall (nearly year-round in mild climates).

HABIT AND GARDEN USE: Upright shrub growing 6'-15' tall and 6'-8' wide. Often massed as a screen; easily sheared as a hedge, but at the expense of some bloom. Also suited to the dry, mixed border.

HOW TO GROW: Prefers full sun in coastal areas, partial shade in hot, dry regions. Drought tolerant once established, but looks better with regular watering. Tolerates most soil types, except those high in alkalinity. Pinch back the tips after flowering to keep the plants compact. No serious pests or diseases.

CULTIVARS AND RELATED SPECIES
E. x *exoniensis* 'Frades' — Compact grower 5'-6' tall; produces many clear pink to rose flowers.

Escallonia rubra, a fast-growing evergreen shrub

OUTSTANDING FEATURES: Spectacular red fall color that is effective over a long period of time. Almost unrivaled for its handsome foliage, brilliant fall leaf color and all-around durability.

HABIT AND GARDEN USE: This deciduous shrub is somewhat vase-shaped with broad-spreading branches. Size is 12'-15' with an equal or greater spread; easily kept smaller with pruning. Leaves are blue-green in summer, becoming crimson red in autumn. Branches on some plants exhibit prominent corky wings, offering considerable winter interest. For use in hedging and screening, as a mass or in the shrub border. An incredibly versatile, attractive shrub.

HOW TO GROW: Burning bush is easily transplanted either from containers or balled and burlapped. It is adaptable to all but wet soils. It also tolerates full sun to full shade, although fall color will be less intense in shadier areas. No serious pest or disease problems.

CULTIVARS AND RELATED SPECIES
'Compactus' — A more compact form of the species that grows to 10' with an equal spread at maturity. Does not exhibit the winged branches, but other traits are similar.

Burning Bush

NATIVE HABITAT
Northeastern Asia to central China

HARDINESS ZONE
USDA 4-9
Sunset 1-9, 14-16

Spectacular fall color

Euonymus alatus, an all-around durable shrub

Border Forsythia

NATIVE HABITAT
Hybrid

HARDINESS ZONE
USDA 5-9
Sunset 2-16,
18-19

Forsythia x *intermedia* in bloom

OUTSTANDING FEATURES: Blooms in early spring in areas where the flower buds are hardy. Bright yellow flowers borne in clusters along the long arching stems literally obscure the plant. Remarkable for its durability as well as adaptability.

HABIT AND GARDEN USE: Habit generally is upright with arching branches; however, some forms are quite pendulous. Best reserved for hedges and massing or used in the shrub border. For use in larger landscapes where plants will be allowed to retain their natural form with minimal pruning.

HOW TO GROW: Border forsythia transplants easily bare root, from containers or balled and burlapped. Adaptable to a wide range of soil types in full sun to full shade, although flowering is reduced in anything less than full sun. Prune immediately after flowering either by cutting to the ground or by selectively removing older canes. No serious insect or disease problems.

CULTIVARS AND RELATED SPECIES

'Spectabilis', Showy Border Forsythia — Rich, bright yellow flowers on a plant 10' in height with an equal spread.

'Lynwood' ('Lynwood Gold') — A sport of 'Spectabilis' with bright yellow flowers that are slightly paler than those of 'Spectabilis'. Growth habit is upright.

F. x 'New Hampshire Gold' — Drooping, single yellow flowers that are relatively cold-hardy. Size is 5' with an equal spread.

F. x 'Northern Sun' — Reliably hardy. Size is 8'-10' with an equal spread.

F. x 'Sunrise' — Cold-hardy, bright yellow flowers. Size is 5' with an equal spread.

OUTSTANDING FEATURES: This striking deciduous shrub will reach 2'-3' in height with a 3' spread. Grown for its fragrant white flowers, borne in 1"-2" terminal spikes in April and May. Foliage is a soothing, glaucous blue in summer; in autumn, it turns yellow and red.

HABIT AND GARDEN USE: Use in foundation plantings, in masses or combined with perennials in the mixed border. A choice addition to smaller gardens because of its diminutive size and long season of interest.

HOW TO GROW: Dwarf fothergilla transplants well balled and burlapped or from a container. It prefers an acid, moist, well-drained soil but is adaptable to many soil types except alkaline ones. Best in full sun to partial shade; tolerates full shade but flowering and fall color will be affected. No serious pests or diseases.

CULTIVARS AND RELATED SPECIES

'Blue Mist' — This cultivar is distinguished by its summer leaves, which are even more blue than those of the species.

'Mount Airy' — Striking and consistently good orange-red fall color is this cultivar's most notable feature.

F. major, Large Fothergilla — Similar to *F. gardenii* but larger.

Dwarf Fothergilla

NATIVE HABITAT
North Carolina to southern Alabama and Florida

HARDINESS ZONE
USDA 4-9
Sunset 3-9, 14-17

The white flowers are fragrant.

Fothergilla gardenii, native to the Southeast

Fremontodendron californicum

Common Flannel Bush

OUTSTANDING FEATURES: Eye-catching, lemon yellow, 1"-2"-wide flowers will stop you dead in your tracks! Saucer-shaped blooms cover shrub all at once between May and June in western regions. Leathery dark green leaves, usually triple-lobed, are covered with brown felt underneath and are a nice foil for the flowers.

NATIVE HABITAT
California

HARDINESS ZONE
USDA 9-10
Sunset 7-24

HABIT AND GARDEN USE: A fast grower, but short-lived in garden settings. Grows 6'-20' tall. Usually upright with a conical to pyramidal form. Best planted alone as a focal point or grouped with other drought-tolerant shrubs (like *Ceanothus*) in drier regions of the garden.

HOW TO GROW: Excellent drainage is a must; hillsides and slopes are ideal. Requires little to no summer water once established, especially in heavy soils (summer irrigation is its downfall). Young plants often require staking. Fungal diseases and root rot can be a problem in overly moist sites.

CULTIVARS AND RELATED SPECIES
'California Glory' — More than 20' tall, with a profusion of 3"-diameter, rich yellow flowers tinged with reddish orange on the outside.

Fremontodendron californicum blooms profusely in May and June.

OUTSTANDING FEATURES: Double white flowers with the most exquisite, intoxicating fragrance. Extremely handsome lustrous, leathery, bright, evergreen leaves.

HABIT AND GARDEN USE: A dense, rounded shrub 4'-6' tall with an equal spread when grown in the ground; smaller in containers. Useful as a hedge, espalier or standard; makes an excellent houseplant in colder regions.

HOW TO GROW: Requires summer heat to grow and bloom well (even as a container plant); likes full sun to partial shade. Particular about acid, moist, well-drained, highly organic soils. Feed every 3-4 weeks during growing season with an acid amendment such as coffee grounds, fish emulsion or blood meal.

CULTIVARS AND RELATED SPECIES
'August Beauty' — A heavy bloomer with large double flowers. Grows 4'-6' tall.

Common Gardenia

NATIVE HABITAT
China

HARDINESS ZONE
USDA 8-10
Sunset 7-9, 12-16, 18-23

Gardenia augusta

The flowers are intoxicatingly fragrant.

Witchhazel

NATIVE HABITAT
Hybrid

HARDINESS ZONE
USDA 5-8
Sunset 4-7,
15-19

H. x *i.* 'Arnold Promise'

OUTSTANDING FEATURES: Unrivaled for dependable winter flowering. Flower colors range from yellows and orange to reds and reddish purple. Fall foliage colors can be a kaleidoscope of yellow, orange and red on the same plant.

HABIT AND GARDEN USE: Depending on the variety, habit is generally upright and spreading with an ultimate size of about 10'-15' in height with an equal or greater spread. For use as a specimen, for massing or combined with evergreens for best flowering effect. Should be located near walkways or windows where it can be enjoyed while in flower.

HOW TO GROW: Transplants best from containers; can be moved balled and burlapped. Prefers moist, acid, well-drained soils in full sun to partial shade. Tolerates full shade but flowering and fall color will be less effective. Resents pruning as wounds do not heal well. Root suckers on grafted plants should be removed regularly. No serious insect or disease problems.

CULTIVARS AND RELATED SPECIES

'Arnold Promise' — Fragrant, clear yellow flowers, among the latest to bloom. Habit is vase-shaped. Fall leaf color is orange-red.

'Diane' — Red flowers and orange-red fall color.

'Jelena' — Outstanding coppery orange flowers borne in profusion along the stems. Fall color is a good orange-red.

H. mollis, Chinese Witchhazel — Among the most dependably fragrant flowers, generally yellow. Native to China.

H. m. 'Pallida' — Fragrant, soft yellow flowers.

H. virginiana, Common Witchhazel — Eastern U.S. native with fragrant yellow flowers in autumn, unfortunately obscured by the foliage. Excellent yellow fall color.

OUTSTANDING FEATURES: An excellent landscape shrub with a rounded, symmetrical form and interesting pattern of small, deep green, 1/3"-long leaves. Hybrid selections offer good flower display. Small spikes of white flowers appear in summer.

HABIT AND GARDEN USE: A fast grower to 5' tall and 3'-5' wide. Good border and boundary shrub, especially in coastal areas subject to wind and salt spray.

HOW TO GROW: Prefers full sun on the coast, partial shade in warmer regions. Good drainage is a must, as well as plenty of moisture. Deadhead and tip prune after flowering to keep plants compact. In southern California and coastal areas of the West, fusarium wilt may cause leaf wilt and dieback — don't replant in infected soils.

Boxleaf Hebe

NATIVE HABITAT
New Zealand

HARDINESS ZONE
USDA 8-9
Sunset 14-24

CULTIVARS AND RELATED SPECIES
'Lake' ('Veronica Lake') — Dense shrub to 3' tall; abundant short spikes of attractive lilac flowers.
'Reevesii' — Two-tone leaves are dark green and reddish purple; reddish purple flower spikes in summer.

Hebe buxifolia has a rounded, symmetrical form and dense, textural foliage.

Rose-of-Sharon

NATIVE HABITAT
Europe, western and northern China

HARDINESS ZONE
USDA 5-9
Sunset 1-21

Hibiscus syriacus 'Diana'

OUTSTANDING FEATURES: Dependable flowering and a long season of bloom account for the long-time popularity of Rose-of-Sharon. Large, showy flowers in a range of colors are borne from mid-summer into fall.

HABIT AND GARDEN USE: A deciduous shrub with erect branches but a bushy habit, up to 8' or more in height and not quite as wide. Foliage is dark, glossy green. A good plant for massing and hedges, or as an addition to the shrub border, where it is valued for its late-season flowers.

HOW TO GROW: Easy to grow; prefers moist, well-drained soils in full sun to partial shade. Adaptable to a range of soil pHs. Pruning to remove dead wood as well as to maintain size is best done in early spring; plants may be cut to within 6" of the ground for rejuvenation at that time. Look for triploid cultivars that produce as few "weed seeds" as possible. No serious pests or diseases.

CULTIVARS AND RELATED SPECIES

U.S. National Arboretum Hybrids — Selected by the U.S. National Arboretum for being triploids, which produce no unwanted "weed seeds":
'Aphrodite' — Large, 4-1/2"-5", dark pink flowers with a prominent red eye.
'Diana' — Large, 4-1/2"-5" pure white flowers that remain open at night.
'Helene' — White flowers with a reddish purple blush at base.
'Minerva' — 4"-5" lavender flowers with a dark red center.

H. rosa sinensis, Hawaiian Hibiscus — Subtropical and tropical shrub with 2"-5"-diameter flowers in various shades of white, red, yellow and orange.

OUTSTANDING FEATURES: A shrub for all seasons: Large, showy, cone-shaped clusters of white flowers appear in early summer. The flowers become pinkish purple as they age and persist for several weeks. Fall color is a mix of reds, orangeish brown and purple and is effective into early winter. Winter stems are an attractive shade of brown; older stems exfoliate to expose a darker, reddish brown interior.

HABIT AND GARDEN USE: Upright, sparsely branched, multi-stemmed shrub 4'-6' in height with an equal or greater spread. Leaves are oak-like, 3"-8" long, resulting in a rather coarse-textured shrub. A good plant for massing, shrub or mixed borders and natural gardens.

Oakleaf Hydrangea

NATIVE HABITAT
Georgia, Florida and Mississippi

HARDINESS ZONE
USDA 5-9
Sunset 1-22

HOW TO GROW: Transplant from containers or balled and burlapped in early spring; in more northern areas protect young plants in winter with burlap until they're established. Prefers moist, well-drained soils high in organic matter in full sun to partial shade. Flowering and fall color will be reduced in full shade. Prune immediately after flowering. No serious pests or diseases.

CULTIVARS AND RELATED SPECIES

'Snow Queen' — Denser bright white flowerheads that fade to pink as they mature. Fall leaf color is reddish bronze.

H. macrophylla, Bigleaf Hydrangea — This old-fashioned hydrangea produces large, round flower clusters in white, pinks and blues; flower color may be dependent on soil pH. Best in coastal areas and in the southern part of its hardiness range (USDA Zones 6-9, Sunset zones 17-21).

Hydrangea quercifolia 'Snowflake', a cultivar with big, double flowers

Virginia Sweetspire

NATIVE HABITAT
New Jersey to Florida
west to Missouri and
Louisiana

HARDINESS ZONE
USDA 5-9
Sunset 1-21

OUTSTANDING FEATURES: Showy white flower clusters 2"-6" long in early summer. Flowers are slightly fragrant and persist for 2-3 weeks. Fall color is variable, ranging from orange and red to dark purple.

HABIT AND GARDEN USE: This suckering deciduous shrub has a rounded habit and will reach 6' with an 8' spread. Summer foliage is dark green and handsome. Excellent as a specimen, or for massing, shrub borders and wet soils. Valuable for its showy flowers at a time when little else is in bloom.

HOW TO GROW: Easily transplanted from a container. Prefers moist, fertile soils in full sun, but tolerates drier soils and shade. In the wild, grows in quite wet areas in full sun and shade. No serious pest or disease problems.

CULTIVARS AND RELATED SPECIES
'Henry's Garnet' — A cultivar distinguished by its showy 6"-long chains of white flowers in June and July. Foliage turns wine-red in fall and persists for several weeks.

Itea virginica 'Henry's Garnet', a cultivar with long chains of white flowers.

OUTSTANDING FEATURES: Among the most spectacular of our eastern North American native plants. The plants are literally obscured by the flowers when in bloom. Attractive, dark, glossy, evergreen foliage provides year-round interest. A choice garden plant when its cultural requirements are met.

Mountain-laurel

HABIT AND GARDEN USE: When given adequate space, mountain laurel tends to be rounded, 6'-12' in height with an equal spread. Plants develop a more irregular form as they age. The bell-shaped flowers in large clusters range in color from pure white to pink to red and appear in early summer. Mountain laurel is an excellent plant for combining with other broadleaved evergreens, as well as for massing, shrub borders, naturalistic gardens and rocky slopes.

NATIVE HABITAT
Quebec and
New Brunswick to
Florida west to Ohio
and Tennessee

HARDINESS ZONE
USDA 4-9
Sunset 1-7, 16-17

HOW TO GROW: Transplants easily from containers or balled and burlapped. Requires a moist, acid, well-drained soil high in organic matter. Will grow in full sun to full shade, although flowering is increased in sun. Pests and diseases include leaf spot, mites, scale and lacebug, most of which can be avoided with proper attention to site selection and adequate moisture.

CULTIVARS AND RELATED SPECIES
'Ostbo Red' — Buds are bright red and become a soft, deep pink when they open.
'Richard Jaynes' — Raspberry-red buds open to reveal pink flowers with a silvery white sheen on the inside.
'Silver Dollar' — Pale pink buds open into extremely large flowers 1-1/2 times the size of those typical of the species.

A red-budded form of *Kalmia latifolia,* native to the eastern U.S.

Japanese Kerria

OUTSTANDING FEATURES: A remarkably pest-free and highly adaptable deciduous shrub. An excellent candidate for city gardens. Spring brings bright yellow flowers for 2-3 weeks, followed by sporadic flowering throughout the season. Bright green stems provide winter interest.

NATIVE HABITAT
Central and western China

HABIT AND GARDEN USE: Arching stems will reach 3'-6' in height with an equal spread; habit is rounded. Flowers are bright yellow, 1-1/2"-1-3/4" across and appear in early spring, continuing sporadically throughout summer. A good plant for massing or combining with other shrubs. Worthwhile for its durability alone.

HARDINESS ZONE
USDA 4-9
Sunset 1-21

HOW TO GROW: Kerria is easily transplanted from a container. The plant prefers moist, fertile soils in full sun to partial shade but will tolerate drier soils and full shade. A widely adaptable shrub. Older stems should be pruned out to help this shrub maintain its vigor. No serious pest or disease problems.

Double-flowered *K.j.* 'Pleniflora'

CULTIVARS AND RELATED SPECIES
'Kinkan' — Stems have yellow and green stripes; flowers are single and yellow.
'Picta' — Leaves are variegated with white edges; flowers are single and yellow.
'Pleniflora' — Yellow flowers are double; the flowers are effective for a longer period than those of the single types.

The species has single flowers.

Kerria japonica is a pest-free, adaptable shrub.

OUTSTANDING FEATURES: Named cultivars produce extremely showy, single flowers in spring that look like tiny roses in white, pink and red (the true species is of little garden interest). Tiny, needle-like leaves vary from dark green to gray-green and are fragrant when bruised. Persistent, woody, long-lasting seed capsules are also of interest.

New Zealand Tea

HABIT AND GARDEN USE: Shrub with a soft, casual, compact habit growing to 6'-12' tall, depending on the cultivar. A useful structural shrub; excellent in mixed borders or containers.

NATIVE HABITAT
New Zealand

HARDINESS ZONE
USDA 9-10
Sunset 14-24

HOW TO GROW: Needs well-drained soils for vigorous root systems and full sun. Water only until plants are established. Responds to shearing; cut selectively back to side branches, never bare wood! No serious pests or diseases.

Red 'Ruby Glow' blooms

CULTIVARS AND RELATED SPECIES
'Helene Strybing' — Large, deep pink flowers and gray-green foliage.
'Ruby Glow' — Compact shrub 6'-8' tall; double, oxblood-red flowers.

Leptospermum scoparium 'Ruby Glow'

Texas Ranger

OUTSTANDING FEATURES: Distinctive, silvery white, evergreen foliage on a compact shrub most suited for desert regions with acid soils. Showy, violet-purple, 1"-long, bell-shaped summer flowers.

HABIT AND GARDEN USE: Grows very compactly to 6'-8' tall and wide. Useful as a rounded, gray foliage mass in dry shrub borders or clipped as a hedge. In humid, warm-night regions of the country, use as a seasonal foliage plant in perennial borders.

NATIVE HABITAT

Texas, New Mexico, Mexico

HOW TO GROW: Tolerates heat, cold, arid conditions and extended periods of drought. Prefers good drainage and suffers in heavy, wet soils, where root rot and fungal diseases can be a problem.

HARDINESS ZONE

USDA 8-9
Sunset 7-24

CULTIVARS AND RELATED SPECIES

'Compactum' — Dense mound 3'-4' in size; orchid-pink flowers.
'Green Cloud' — Deep violet flowers and distinctive dark green foliage.
'White Cloud' — Silvery leaves and white flowers.

Leucophyllum frutescens has silvery foliage and showy summer blooms.

OUTSTANDING FEATURES: Japanese privet is one of the most durable broadleaved evergreens for hedges and screening. Its lustrous, dark green, leathery foliage tolerates pruning well. Adapts well to urban conditions. Tolerates a wide range of soil types and exposures.

HABIT AND GARDEN USE: Left unpruned, this privet tends to be dense, upright and somewhat rounded. It grows to 6'-15' in height with a smaller spread. Typically, however, plants are tightly pruned and used for hedging, foundation plantings or topiary.

HOW TO GROW: Japanese privet transplants readily bare root. It is not fussy about soil types or exposures, although plants grown in full shade tend to become leggy and unkempt. Pests and diseases include leaf spot, powdery mildew, scale and spider mite; however, none of these problems seem to affect the plant to any great extent.

CULTIVARS AND RELATED SPECIES

L. amurense, Amur Privet — Used extensively for hedging in the North (USDA Zones 3-7), where it is dependably cold hardy. Deciduous.

L. lucidum, Glossy Privet — Very similar to amur privet, but with larger flower and fruit clusters.

Japanese
Privet

NATIVE HABITAT
Japan

HARDINESS ZONE
USDA 7-10
Sunset 4-24

L. lucidum in fruit

Ligustrum japonicum is usually used as a hedge.

Fragrant or Winter Honeysuckle

NATIVE HABITAT
Eastern China

HARDINESS ZONE
USDA 4-8
Sunset 1-9, 14-24

The fragrant flowers last for weeks.

OUTSTANDING FEATURES: Extremely fragrant white flowers borne in profusion along the stems. Flowers appear in late winter and early spring and are effective for several weeks. Among the most fragrant of earliest-blooming shrubs.

HABIT AND GARDEN USE: Tends to be wide-spreading with long, arching branches. Younger plants are rounded; older ones, more tree-like. Foliage is bluish green in summer and persists late into the season; may tend to be evergreen in the more southern part of its hardiness range. A good plant for hedges and screening, the shrub border or limbed up and used as a small multi-stemmed tree. Should be located near walkways or other areas where the fragrance can be readily enjoyed. Branches are good for forcing in winter.

HOW TO GROW: Winter honeysuckle is easily transplanted from a container or balled and burlapped. It tolerates a wide range of soil types and pH in full sun to partial shade. Pests and diseases include leafspot, powdery mildew, aphids and mealybugs, although none are serious.

CULTIVARS AND RELATED SPECIES
Lonicera pileata, Privet Honeysuckle — A low-growing shrub only 2'-3' in height and twice as wide. Foliage is evergreen, dark and glossy. Flowers and fruit are insignificant. Most often used as a groundcover and because of its durability.

Lonicera fragrantissima blooms in late winter.

OUTSTANDING FEATURES: A tiered, evergreen shrub with subtle beauty. Its oval leaves are 1"-2" long and dark green; new growth is contrasting lime green. A profusion of spidery, mildly fragrant white flowers with 4 narrow, twisted petals appear in clusters at the ends of branches from March to April in mild-winter regions and sporadically throughout the season. A shrub that deserves more recognition.

HABIT AND GARDEN USE: Generally a rather neat, compact shrub with tiered, cascading branches, 3'-5' tall and just as wide. Good in the front of mixed borders with room to sprawl, in raised beds and planter boxes, rock and hillside gardens and hanging baskets.

HOW TO GROW: Prefers full sun in foggy, overcast coastal areas; partial shade in warmer inland regions. Needs rich, organic, well-drained soil and ample moisture. Allow to grow naturally with little pruning for best form. No serious pests or diseases.

CULTIVARS AND RELATED SPECIES
'Burgundy' — A bright, pinkish rose-flowered form with purple foliage.

NATIVE HABITAT
China

HARDINESS ZONE
USDA 8-9
Sunset 6-9, 14-24

Loropetalum chinense

The spidery flowers are mildly fragrant.

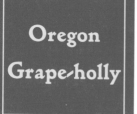

Oregon Grape-holly

NATIVE HABITAT
British Columbia to
northern California

HARDINESS ZONE
USDA 4-8
Sunset 1-21

OUTSTANDING FEATURES: A glossy evergreen shrub with compound, spiny, holly-like leaves and an architectural growth habit. New growth is reddish bronze and contrasts nicely with older branches. Bright yellow flowers in 2"-3"-long clusters appear from March to May, followed by edible bluish black berries that are covered with a powdery gray coating and attract birds.

HABIT AND GARDEN USE: Sparsely branched with an irregular, upright form 3'-6' tall by 3'-5' wide. Spreads by underground shoots. Ideal planted in masses in natural woodland settings or as a low screen or barrier shrub; also a good accent plant alone or in mixed borders.

HOW TO GROW: Looks best when grown in shade. Prefers moist, well-drained, acid soils; leaves may be yellow and chlorotic in high-pH soils. Shelter from hot, dry winds. Prune out long, bare, woody stems for a more uniform, compact shape. Small looper caterpillars that skeletonize the leaves can be troublesome.

CULTIVARS AND RELATED SPECIES
'Compactum' — Handsome, dwarf form with glossy foliage, 2'-3' in height.
M. lomariifolia — Vertical habit; 6'-10' tall with leaves clustered at branch ends. Yellow flower clusters mature to powdery blue berries. Very architectural.

Mahonia aquifolium, with its grape-like fruit clusters and holly-like leaves

OUTSTANDING One of the most useful, basic evergreen shrubs in mild climates. Pointed, bright green, 2" leaves are strongly aromatic and reminiscent of the Mediterranean region. Summertime brings white, sweetly-scented, 3/4" flowers with many stamens, followed by small, bluish black berries.

HABIT AND GARDEN USE: A rounded form reaching 5'-6' high and 4'-5' wide; older specimens can attain the proportions of small trees. One of the best shrubs for formal hedges and screens. Single specimens can be "limbed up" to reveal attractive bark and branching structure.

HOW TO GROW: Grows well in part shade to full sun. Not particular about soil type, but demands good drainage. Leaf chlorosis may result in poorly drained soils. No serious pests or diseases.

CULTIVARS AND RELATED SPECIES
'Compacta' — Slow-growing, compact plant with densely set, small leaves; an excellent low edging shrub.

Greek Myrtle

NATIVE HABITAT
Mediterranean region

HARDINESS ZONE
USDA 9-10
Sunset 8-24

The flowers are sweetly scented.

Myrtus communis makes a handsome evergreen hedge.

Heavenly bamboo

NATIVE HABITAT
China

HARDINESS ZONE
USDA 6-9
Sunset 5-24

Nandina domestica

OUTSTANDING FEATURES: A valuable addition to any garden for its unusually fine texture, showy flowers and fruit, as well as its brilliantly colored foliage throughout the year.

HABIT AND GARDEN USE: Distinctly upright in habit; foliage arises from arching canes. The species will reach 6'-8' in height with an equal spread; there are dozens of cultivars, however, some of which reach only a few inches in height. Foliage is extremely fine-textured, graceful and dark, glossy green in summer, becoming reddish purple in fall. Evergreen in all except the most northern part of its hardiness range. The white flowers are borne in large terminal clusters in mid-summer and are followed by orangish red fruit in fall. A good plant for screening, the shrub border or as a groundcover when the low-growing cultivars are used.

HOW TO GROW: Generally transplanted from containers. Prefers moist soil in full sun but is widely adaptable to soil types and exposures. No serious pests or diseases.

CULTIVARS AND RELATED SPECIES
'Gulf Stream' — A cultivar distinguished by its bluish-green summer color and brilliant red winter color. Growth habit is compact, reaching only 2-1/2'-3-1/2' in height with an equal spread.
'Harbor Dwarf' — One of the best dwarf forms; grows only 2'-3' in height and width. Foliage is red in winter.
'Yellow Fruited' — Prized for its yellow fruits. Similar to the species in all other aspects.
'San Gabriel' ('Filamentosa') — This cultivar has very narrow, fine-textured leaves, producing an overall ferny appearance.

OUTSTANDING FEATURES: One of the last hardy shrubs to bloom in the fall. Numerous small white flowers are borne in the axils of the leaves in October and November. Flowers, for the most part, are obscured by the dense foliage, but their strong sweet fragrance permeates the air. The dark, glossy foliage is evergreen and similar in appearance to some hollies, hence the common name.

HABIT AND GARDEN USE: Dense and rounded, forming an impenetrable mass 8'-10' in height with an equal or smaller spread. Provides year-round interest with its attractive evergreen foliage and late flowering. An excellent choice for hedging, as a screen or as a specimen.

HOW TO GROW: Transplants easily from containers. Prefers a moist, acid, well-drained soil in full sun to partial shade. Should be protected from winter sun and wind in the northern parts of its hardiness range. Tolerates urban conditions. No serious pests or diseases.

CULTIVARS AND RELATED SPECIES
'Gulftide' — A compact, cold-hardy form.
'Rotundifolius' — A dwarf form that lacks the spiny leaf margins. Slow growing and less cold tolerant than the species.
'Variegatus' — A variegated form of the species with creamy white leaf margins. Less cold hardy than the species.
O. x *fortunei*, Fortune's Osmanthus — A hybrid between *O. heterophyllus* and *O. fragrans*. Larger and more vigorous than the holly osmanthus, but also less hardy. Flowers are exceedingly fragrant — excessively so on larger plants. Hardy in USDA Zones 8 and 9; Sunset Zones 5-10, 14-24.

Holly Osmanthus

NATIVE HABITAT
Japan

HARDINESS ZONE
USDA 7-9
Sunset 3-10, 14-24

Osmanthus heterophyllus

Sweet Mockorange

NATIVE HABITAT
Southeastern Europe
and Asia Minor

HARDINESS ZONE
USDA 4-8
Sunset 1-17

Philadelphus coronarius

OUTSTANDING FEATURES: An old-fashioned favorite beloved for its extremely fragrant flowers, which appear in early summer. Some of the newer hybrids and cultivars offer compact habit in addition to the sweet fragrance.

HABIT AND GARDEN USE: The species is a large, gangly shrub 10'-12' with an equal spread. Stems tend to be upright and stiff, and frequently are bare along the base. Flowers are 1"-1-1/2" across and borne in racemes in early summer. Best reserved for the shrub or mixed border.

HOW TO GROW: Transplants readily into a wide range of soil types and exposures, although best flowering occurs in full sun. Prune after flowering to control size and maintain habit. Periodically, plants should be cut to the ground for rejuvenation. No serious pests or diseases.

CULTIVARS AND RELATED SPECIES

'Miniature Snowflake' — Grows to 3' tall. Double, fragrant flowers.

P. x 'Snowgoose' — Selected for extremely fragrant, white, double flowers borne in profusion. Size is 4'-5' with a spread that is half as wide.

P. x *lemoinei* 'Avalanche' — Single white flowers 1" across and very fragrant. Size is 4' tall with an equal spread.

P. x *lemoinei* 'Belle Etoile' — Flowers are fragrant, single, white and 2-1/4" across with a purple blotch. Size is 6' high with a smaller spread.

P. x *virginalis* 'Minnesota Snowflake' — Double white flowers 2" in diameter are produced on plants that will reach 8' in height with branches to the ground.

OUTSTANDING FEATURES: Grown for the eye-catching, bright red color of the new foliage. Mature, faded leaves are a glossy dark green and vary from 2"-5" long. White flower clusters are not particularly showy and are usually sheared off.

HABIT AND GARDEN USE: A fast grower to 10'-15' tall with a wider spread. Good for screens and hedges and as background plants — there's nothing quite like a hedge of photinia with the sun backlighting its brilliant reddish foliage.

HOW TO GROW: A good, tough plant in almost any soil. Likes full sun, but tolerates some shade. A troublesome leaf spot may develop in moist, humid regions.

Fraser Photinia

NATIVE HABITAT
Hybrid

HARDINESS ZONE
USDA 8-9
Sunset 4-24

CULTIVARS AND RELATED SPECIES
'Indian Princess' — Compact, dense, slower-growing plant, 5'-6' tall; new foliage is more orange than red.

Photinia x *fraseri* forms a backdrop for Japanese anemones.

Mountain Andromeda

NATIVE HABITAT
Japan

HARDINESS ZONE
USDA 5-8
(borderline 4)
Sunset 1-9, 14-17

Pieris japonica

OUTSTANDING FEATURES: An exceptional evergreen shrub with a refined, neat form and attractive foliage and flowers. Flower buds in early winter look like strings of tiny, greenish pink beads and open to pendulous clusters of white, lily-of-the-valley-like flowers that impart a light fragrance from March to April. New, bronzy pink to red leaf growth sets this shrub aglow in spring.

HABIT AND GARDEN USE: Grows 9'-12' in height, spreading 6'-8'. Produces a rather stiff, dense shape with a layered, tiered effect. This excellent, broadleaved evergreen works well in the shrub border, naturalistic woodland garden and massed with other evergreens for screening and background.

HOW TO GROW: Demands moist, acid, well-drained soil high in organic matter. Best in partial shade; lace bugs and mites can be troublesome in full sun. Prune after flowering and protect from the wind. Responds well to frequent feeding, especially in high-rainfall areas, where leaching of nutrients can cause leaf yellowing.

CULTIVARS AND RELATED SPECIES

'Christmas Cheer' — Flowers are pink with deeper pink tips, producing a bicolor appearance.

'Dorothy Wycoff' — Compact form with dark red flower buds that open to white.

'Mountain Fire' — New foliage is an exceptional fire red; flowers are white.

'Valley Valentine' — Rich maroon flower buds become long-lasting, deep rose-pink flowers.

P.j. 'Dorothy Wycoff', with dark red flowerbuds that open to white

OUTSTANDING FEATURES: Valued for clean-looking, leathery, evergreen foliage. The lustrous, dark green leaves are 2"-5" long and rounded at the ends. Clusters of creamy white flowers at the branch tips smell like orange blossoms in spring. Round green fruits turn brown in the fall and split to reveal orange seeds.

Japanese Pittosporum

HABIT AND GARDEN USE: A dense, compact, broad-spreading shrub from 6'-12' tall with a 15'-20' spread. Excellent for screening, massing and buffer and barrier plantings — although it is overused in south Florida and California. A single specimen sited where its fragrance can be savored can't be beat! Also makes a good container shrub.

NATIVE HABITAT
Japan, Korea, China

HARDINESS ZONE
USDA 8-10
Sunset 8-24

HOW TO GROW: Very adaptable to a variety of soil types from sand to clay, as long as there is good drainage. Thrives in hot, dry locations; tolerates full sun, shade and salt spray. Relatively easy to head back and thin branches to control size. No serious pests and diseases.

CULTIVARS AND RELATED SPECIES
'Variegata' — Gray-green leaves edged with white; smaller, lower-growing to 5' tall.
'Wheeler's Dwarf' — Compact, mounded form 3' to 4' tall and wide with smaller
   leaves, stems and flowers.

Pittosporum tobira is prized for its lustrous, dark green leaves.

Bush Cinquefoil

NATIVE HABITAT
Northern Hemisphere

HARDINESS ZONE
USDA 2-7
Sunset 1-21

Potentilla fruticosa 'Goldfinger'

OUTSTANDING FEATURES: Among the longest blooming of shrubs that can be grown in the north. Flowers are small, 1" across but are borne in profusion along the branches. Color ranges from white and pink to red, orange and yellow. Flowering begins in early summer and continues until frost. Compact habit adds to its appeal for a wide variety of landscape uses.

HABIT AND GARDEN USE: Habit is upright and slender. Branches tend to arch as they age, resulting in a mounded form. Size ranges from 1'-4' in height with a similar spread. Foliage can be bright green to bluish green in color, depending on the cultivar being grown. A choice plant for foundation plantings, mixed borders and smaller gardens because of its compact habit and long season of bloom. Can be massed or used for a low hedge.

HOW TO GROW: Bush cinquefoil does best in the northern part of its hardiness range; high nighttime temperatures seem to limit its performance in warmer areas. Transplants easily from containers or balled and burlapped. Thrives in moist soils in full sun but tolerates dry and alkaline soils. Remove one third of the older canes in late winter or before growth begins in spring to maintain vigor. No serious pests or diseases, although powdery mildew may appear late in the season.

CULTIVARS AND RELATED SPECIES
'Abbotswood' — Pure white flowers and blue-green foliage. Grows 3' tall and wide.
'Goldfinger' — Large 1-1/2" to 1-3/4" yellow flowers on compact plants 3' to 4' tall and wide.
'Tangerine' — 1-1/4" flowers are yellow infused with orangish red. Mounded habit 2' to 4' in height.

OUTSTANDING FEATURES: A popular broadleaved evergreen that performs admirably for hedging or combining with other shrubs, especially broadleaved evergreens. Makes a nice evergreen showing in shade where little else will grow.

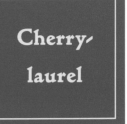

Cherry-laurel

HABIT AND GARDEN USE: A large, wide-spreading evergreen shrub reaching 10' in height with a greater spread. Can easily be kept smaller with minimal pruning. Foliage is dense, glossy, dark green. The small white flowers are fragrant and appear in 2"-5" clusters in late spring. Fruit is black and generally is obscured by the leaves. A good plant for difficult shady areas; excellent for hedging.

NATIVE HABITAT
SE Europe, Asia Minor

HARDINESS ZONE
USDA 6-8
Sunset 4-9, 14-24

HOW TO GROW: Transplants easily from containers or balled and burlapped. Prefers a moist, well-drained soil high in organic matter. Does well in full to partial shade. Withstands heavy pruning. Pests and diseases include root rot and a bacterium that attacks the foliage; both of these can be avoided by planting in well-drained soils. Do not overfertilize.

CULTIVARS AND RELATED SPECIES
'Otto Luyken' — Selected for dwarf size and compact habit. Will reach 3'-4' in height with a spread twice as wide. Flowers heavily even in full shade.
'Schipkaensis — One of the hardiest forms. Reaches 4'-5' in height with a spread of 8'-10'. Flowering is poor in comparison with other cultivars.
'Zabelliana' — A low-growing cultivar reaching only 3' in height with a 9'-12' spread. Good flowering habit.

Prunus laurocerasus 'Otto Luyken'

The flowers are small and fragrant.

Scarlet Firethorn

NATIVE HABITAT
Italy to Caucasus

HARDINESS ZONE
USDA 6-9
Sunset 1-24

Pyracantha x 'Mohave'

OUTSTANDING FEATURES: Almost unrivalled for its fall fruit display. Fruits are borne in large, showy clusters and range in color from pure orange to orange-red to red to yellow. Combines well with surrounding fall foliage and broadleaved evergreens. Fruit can persist well into winter.

HABIT AND GARDEN USE: Habit is variable, depending on the cultivar, though typically stiffly upright. Branches arch with age, becoming open in the center. Size ranges from 6'-18' with an equal spread. Can and should be kept in bounds with regular pruning. For use in the shrub border or for massing and hedges, as it will provide an impenetrable thorny mass. When trained as an espalier, proper pruning will make the most of the fruit display.

HOW TO GROW: Transplanted in spring from a container into well-drained soil in full sun to partial shade. Difficult to transplant once established; therefore choosing the right site initially is important. Prune at almost any time to maintain size and habit. Fireblight and scab can be serious problems, so be sure to look for a resistant cultivar. Aphids, lacebug and scale can also be troublesome if this shrub is not planted in a suitable site.

CULTIVARS AND RELATED SPECIES

'Fiery Cascade' — Upright habit 8'-10' tall and wide. Fruit starts out orange, becomes bright red and persists for weeks. Good disease resistance.

'Rutgers' — A dwarf, low-spreading form reaching 3' tall and 9' wide. Fruit is orange-red and abundant. Hardy and disease resistant.

'Teton' — Unusual, extremely upright growth habit and yellowish orange fruits. Ultimate size is 15' tall and half as wide. Resistant to fireblight and scab.

OUTSTANDING FEATURES: Glossy, leathery, 1"-3" leaves and compact growth and a profusion of white flowers tinged with pink in spring. Dark blue, berry-like fruits follow the flowers but are often not terribly showy.

HABIT AND GARDEN USE: A rounded shrub 4'-5' tall, perfect for background plantings and as low dividers and informal hedges. The species is rarely grown; cutivated varieties are much more commonplace.

HOW TO GROW: Easy-to-grow shrub in full sun. Prefers moist, well-drained soils. Tolerates drought and salt spray in coastal regions, and restricted root space in containers. Occasionally attacked by aphids and plagued by leaf spotting.

Indian Hawthorn

NATIVE HABITAT
China

HARDINESS ZONE
USDA 9-10
Sunset 8-10,
12-24

CULTIVARS AND RELATED SPECIES
'Ballerina' — Vibrant rosy pink flowers; rounded form 3'-4' tall.
'Indian Princess' — Bright pink flowers that fade to white; compact, broad-mounded form.

Rhaphiolepis indica, with pinkish white flowers in spring

Fragrant Sumac

OUTSTANDING FEATURES: A useful shrub for covering large or difficult areas. Tolerates a wide range of soil types and exposures. Plant has a suckering habit, and stems that touch the ground root readily. Both of these attributes make it a good choice for stabilizing banks and massing. Fall color is outstanding and persists for several weeks.

NATIVE HABITAT
Vermont and Ontario to Minnesota south to Louisiana and Florida

HARDINESS ZONE
USDA 3-9
Sunset 1-3, 10

Rhus aromatica, a good groundcover

HABIT AND GARDEN USE: Habit is irregular but generally mounded, 2'-6' in height with a spread of 6'-10'. Foliage is glossy green, becoming a mix of oranges, reds and purples in fall. An excellent choice for a groundcover, used as a facer plant to hide the bases of scraggly shrubs or in the mixed border.

HOW TO GROW: Fragrant sumac transplants easily into a wide range of soil types, although it prefers acid soils. Also tolerates a range of exposures, from full sun to partial shade. Plants can be cut to the ground in early spring if they become overgrown. No serious pests or diseases.

CULTIVARS AND RELATED SPECIES
'Gro-low' — Selected for its low-growing (2'), wide-spreading (6'-8') habit and dependable orange-red fall color.
R. typhina 'Laciniata', Cutleaf Staghorn Sumac — Similar in habit and use to fragrant sumac, although larger. Leaves are 1'-2' long but deeply dissected, giving the shrub a fine-textured appearance. Fall color is brilliant orange-red. Excellent for slopes and massing. Should be cut to the ground annually to maintain appearance and vigor.

Fall color is outstanding and lasts for weeks.

OUTSTANDING FEATURES: A dependable deciduous shrub. Bright green leaves are roundish, 3-5-lobed, toothed on the margins and vary in size from 1"-2" long. Flowers and fruit are inconspicuous.

HABIT AND GARDEN USE: Rounded, dense and twiggy. 3'-6' tall with an equal or broader spread. An excellent hedge plant and useful in informal masses.

HOW TO GROW: Easy to grow in full sun or shade in just about any type of soil. Because the flowers are unremarkable, you can prune anytime to shape and control the shrub. Leaf spot, rust and anthracnose can be serious problems during wet seasons.

CULTIVARS AND RELATED SPECIES

'Aureum' — Dwarf type with yellowish leaves; best in full sun.

'Green Mound' — Dwarf form, 2'-3' high and wide.

R. sanguineum glutinosum, Red-flowering Currant — A deciduous West Coast native with pendulous, pink flowers in late-winter and spring.

Alpine Currant

NATIVE HABITAT
Europe

HARDINESS ZONE
USDA 2-7
Sunset 1-3, 10

Alpine currant in flower

A low hedge of *Ribes alpinum*

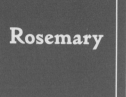

Rosemary

OUTSTANDING FEATURES: Picturesque evergreen shrub for warmer regions with needle-like leaves that emit a potent aroma when bruised. Small clusters of lavender-blue, 1/4"-1/2" flowers bloom most heavily in winter and spring. Leaves are used as seasoning; flowers are very attractive to bees.

NATIVE HABITAT
Europe, Asia Minor

HARDINESS ZONE
USDA 6-9
Sunset 4-24

HABIT AND GARDEN USE: In favorable climates reaches 2'-6' in height and width, depending on the cultivar. Taller varieties are useful as clipped hedges or in mixed, dry borders with gray-leaved plants. Lower types are excellent on banks and slopes or in raised beds and containers, trailing over the edges to make a curtain of green.

HOW TO GROW: Easy to grow, enduring hot sun and poor, gravelly soils with good drainage. A water-thrifty shrub once established, it requires infrequent water and no fertilizing. Withstands tip-pinching, shearing and light pruning. No serious pest or disease problems.

CULTIVARS AND RELATED SPECIES

'Collingwood Ingram' ('Beneden Blue') — Semi-erect habit, 2'-2-1/2' tall, spreading to 4' with branches that curve gracefully to the ground. Flowers are the most vivid gentian-blue.

'Prostratus' — Irregular, trailing habit; 2' tall with 4'-8' spread. Pale lavender-blue flowers.

'Tuscan Blue' — Rigid, upright branches to 6' tall. Clear blue flowers.

Rosmarinus officinalis with its clusters of small lavender-blue flowers

OUTSTANDING FEATURES: This Asian native has long been grown for its large, silver "pussy willows." The silver-white catkins are 1-1/4" when mature and last a long time. This shrub is a great addition to the early-spring garden. Branches can be cut early and brought indoors for forcing.

HABIT AND GARDEN USE: Roseglow pussy willow is lower growing than most of the willows planted for their spring catkins. Its stems are generally upright, 6'-8' in height with an equal or greater spread. Summer foliage is bluish green; fall color is yellow. One of the more manageable willows in the landscape. A nice addition to the shrub border.

Roseglow Pussy Willow

NATIVE HABITAT
Japan and Korea

HARDINESS ZONE
USDA 5-8
Sunset 1-24

HOW TO GROW: Easy to grow. Prefers moist, well-drained soil in full sun. Can grow as much as 4'-6' per year; plant should be cut back hard in order to encourage good stem production. Pruning is best done in winter. Bacterial blight on leaves and shoots, leaf spots, cankers, powdery mildew, scale and spider mites are among the pests and diseases, although none is particularly serious.

CULTIVARS AND RELATED SPECIES
S. gracilistyla melanostachys, Black Pussy Willow — Similar to the above in all respects, except the catkins, which are black with red anthers, create an unusual and striking effect.

Salix gracilistyla with silver catkins, commonly known as pussy willows

Sweetbox

OUTSTANDING FEATURES: An elegant, evergreen shrub with an intoxicating, sweet aroma when in flower. Dark green, glossy, oval, pointed leaves densely cover the branches. Tiny flowers, which are intensely fragrant, bloom in late winter and early spring, followed by blue-black fruits.

NATIVE HABITAT
Himalayas, China

HARDINESS ZONE
USDA 5-8
Sunset 4-9, 14-24

HABIT AND GARDEN USE: This plant grows 18"-24" tall and spreads slowly to 4'-6' or more. More cold tolerant than the species listed below. Of great value in shade gardens, where choice of shrubs is often limited. Its uniformly low growth habit makes it suitable for the foreground of borders and as a ground-cover beneath low-branching trees.

HOW TO GROW: Easy to grow in shade in rich, organic soils topdressed with mulch or compost. Scale insects may attack plants, but can be controlled with horticultural oil sprays.

CULTIVARS AND RELATED SPECIES

S. confusa — A 4'-6' shrub with sweet-smelling flowers that mature to black fruits.

S. ruscifolia — A 4'-6' shrub; wavy evergreen foliage; very fragrant flowers followed by red fruits.

Sarcococca hookeriana humilis has dark green, glossy, evergreen leaves.

OUTSTANDING FEATURES: A popular foliage and flowering shrub in interior desert regions of the Southwest and coastal California. Known for its soft, gray-green, finely divided foliage. Clusters of striking, clear yellow flowers from mid-winter to early spring followed by persistent, 2"-3"-long seed pods.

HABIT AND GARDEN USE: Handsome rounded to mounding shrub, 3'-5' high with an equal spread. Effective when massed on banks as a background for other plantings or as accents in mixed borders.

HOW TO GROW: Needs good drainage in clay soils; requires little water. Prune after flowering to control size. Frost tender. No serious pests or diseases.

Feathery Cassia

NATIVE HABITAT
Australia

HARDINESS ZONE
USDA 9-10
Sunset 8-9, 12-16, 18-23

Senna artemisioides, a handsome flowering shrub for the Desert Southwest

Japanese Skimmia

OUTSTANDING FEATURES: A charming evergreen shrub grown for its fragrant white flowers and showy red fruits. Upright clusters of flowers appear in early spring and are followed in October by crimson fruits that persist through winter.

NATIVE HABITAT
Japan

HARDINESS ZONE
USDA 7
6(with protection)-9

HABIT AND GARDEN USE: Dense and mounded, ultimately reaching 3'-4' tall with a greater spread. Glossy evergreen leaves are 2-1/2"-4" long. Male and female flowers are white, and the female flowers are followed by brilliant red fruits. Excellent for foundation plantings, combined with other broadleaf evergreens and for containers or small, city gardens.

HOW TO GROW: Transplant from containers. Prefers soils that are moist and well-drained, in full to partial shade. Avoid areas exposed to winter sun and drying winds. Until established, this shrub benefits from regular soakings during dry periods. In northern areas, provide winter protection. Somewhat susceptible to mites, which can be avoided by planting in shade and providing adequate moisture. Plants are dioecious (that is, male and female flowers are borne on separate plants); so be sure to plant a pair for fruit set.

CULTIVARS AND RELATED SPECIES

S. reevesiana, Reeves Skimmia — Similar to *S. japonica* except that plants are bisexual; that is, male and female flower parts appear on the same plant and so only a single plant is needed for fruit set. Reeves skimmia also tends to be more compact, 1-1/2'-2' tall with a spread of 2'-3'.

The fruits persist through the winter.

Skimmia japonica flowers are fragrant.

OUTSTANDING FEATURES: An eminently adaptable shrub valued for its hardiness, flower and foliage color as well as its tolerance to a wide range of soil types and exposures. Compact habit and durability make it a good choice for lower-maintenance landscapes.

Bumald Spirea

HABIT AND GARDEN USE: Habit and size tend to vary depending on the cultivar, but generally this shrub is dwarf, compact and well branched. Foliage generally emerges early in spring and in many varieties is pink to wine red. Summer leaf color varies from blue-green to golden yellow and variegated. Fall color ranges from non-existent to mixes of oranges, reds and purples. Flowers are generally white but there are pink- and rose-colored varieties. Use in shrub and mixed borders, foundation plantings and massed.

NATIVE HABITAT
Parent species native to China, Korea and Japan

HARDINESS ZONE
USDA 38
Sunset 1-11, 14-21

HOW TO GROW: Bumald spirea transplants readily. It prefers moist soils but will tolerate all soil types, except wet. This spirea does best in full sun or partial shade. Periodic removal of old stems will help to keep the plant in good condition. Removal of spent flower heads will encourage continued flowering in summer. Spireas are prone to a host of pests and diseases; however, none of them are particularly serious.

Spiraea x *bumalda* 'Golden Princess'

CULTIVARS AND RELATED SPECIES

'Goldflame' — Brilliant leaf color, which begins as a rich reddish orange in early spring and changes to a soft yellow in summer. Fall color is similar to that in early spring, except in cooler climates, where summer leaf color is retained in fall. Flowers are small and brownish pink.

S. japonica 'Alpina', Dwarf Japanese Spirea — A dainty, fine-textured, low-growing shrub with pink flowers. Excellent as a low, foreground hedge or groundcover or cascading over a wall.

S. nipponica 'Snowmound', Snowmound Nippon Spirea — Plant habit is compact, 2-1/2' -3' with an equal spread. White flowers are borne in profusion with the emerging blue-green foliage in early spring.

Stachyurus

NATIVE HABITAT
Japan

HARDINESS ZONE
USDA 6-8
Sunset 4-6, 14-17

Stachyurus praecox

OUTSTANDING FEATURES: In flower, a shrub of mysterious beauty. 3"-4"-long, pendulous chains of pale yellow, papery, bell-shaped flowers bloom in early spring (March to April), well ahead of the nondescript foliage. Polished, chestnut brown branches are a nice complement to the flowers. In leaf the shrub becomes very commonplace, with 3"-7"-long leaves tapering to a sharp point. Fall color is a muted yellow-red.

HABIT AND GARDEN USE: A deciduous shrub growing slowly to 6'-10' in height and width. Upright, arching stems give an overall rounded outline. Useful in a prominent spot in border plantings and near entryways, patios and courtyards where it can be viewed close up.

HOW TO GROW: This shrub is very easy to grow in full sun or light, overhead shade. It prefers soils that are acid and well-drained and with average moisture.

The pendulous chains of bell-shaped flowers bloom in early spring.

OUTSTANDING FEATURES: Held in high esteem for the unforgettable fragrance. Flowers are borne in large terminal clusters at the ends of the branches, come in singles and doubles and range in color from white and pink to rose and purple; even a pale yellow variety has been introduced. Fragrance varies with cultivar from intense to barely perceptible.

Common Lilac

HABIT AND GARDEN USE: Habit tends to be upright and leggy, to 8'-15' in height with an equal or greater spread. Foliage is coarse and generally dark green. On many older cultivars the leaves are susceptible to powdery mildew and become unsightly. Best reserved for the shrub border as most varieties have little to offer once flowering has past.

NATIVE HABITAT
Southern Europe

HARDINESS ZONE
USDA 3-7
Sunset 1-11

HOW TO GROW: Common lilac is easily transplanted in early spring, whether bare root, from containers or balled and burlapped. It does best in moist, near-neutral soils high in organic matter. Spent blooms should be removed immediately after flowering. Periodically, older canes should be pruned to the ground to encourage a more compact plant. Lilacs are prone to numerous pests and diseases. Borers, scale and powdery mildew alone can require considerable attention, so be sure to look for a resistant cultivar.

Syringa vulgaris *'Violetta'*

CULTIVARS AND RELATED SPECIES

There are hundreds of different cultivars of the common lilac. Take the time to select one that is compact, has fragrant flowers and is disease resistant.

S. *meyeri* 'Palibin' — A cultivar of the meyer lilac distinguished by its compact habit (4'-5' high and 5'-7' wide) and showy blooms. Reddish purple buds open to whitish pink flowers before the leaves grow large and they are obscured. One of the best smaller lilacs.

Tamarisk

OUTSTANDING FEATURES: Valued for its fine-textured, ferny foliage and showy blooms in early summer. Flowers are small, rosy pink and borne in short clusters that combine to make a flowering mass up to 3' in length. After flowering, the airy foliage offers a cool, tropical effect. An excellent choice for poor sandy soils, particularly near the shore.

NATIVE HABITAT
Southeastern Europe to Central Asia

HABIT AND GARDEN USE: Irregular, open-growing shrub 10'-15' tall and as wide. If left unpruned, the plant can develop into a small tree but generally looks unkempt. Best reserved for difficult sites in full sun on poor soil.

HARDINESS ZONE
USDA 2-8
Sunset 1-24

HOW TO GROW: Best transplanted from containers, as root systems tend to be poor. Requires soils low in fertility in full sun; otherwise growth will become rank. Disease and pest problems can be prevented by choosing a suitable site.

The blooms appear in early summer.

Tamarix ramosissima, a good choice for poor soils

OUTSTANDING FEATURES: Vivid, velvety, royal-purple, 3"-diameter flowers make this shrub an outstanding addition to gardens in warm regions. Branch tips, buds and new growth are covered with reddish orange hairs. The velvety green leaves are oval-shaped, 3"-6" long and strongly veined. Older leaves add spots of red, orange or yellow in any season before dropping.

HABIT AND GARDEN USE: Fast-growing, 5'-18' high and 5' -10' wide, with an open appearance. A marvelous ever-green shrub for the mixed border, especially where it can be backlit. Also suitable for containers.

HOW TO GROW: Princess flower is generally easy to grow in somewhat acid, well-drained soils. It likes its roots in the shade and top in the sun. Needs some supplemental water and protection from winds. A tendency toward legginess is prevented by pinching back the branch tips, especially when the shrub is young, and by deadheading spent flowers. Will resprout after heavy pruning. Feed lightly after each bloom cycle. Flower buds may be prone to tobacco budworm.

Princess Flower

NATIVE HABITAT
Brazil

HARDINESS ZONE
USDA 9-10
Sunset 16-17, 21-24

Tibouchina urvilleana

The velvety purple flowers are 3 inches wide.

Korean Spice Viburnum

OUTSTANDING FEATURES: A truly outstanding shrub for fragrance! Rounded clusters of pink to reddish buds open to white, 1/2" flowers in late April to early May. Deciduous leaves are round-pointed, irregularly toothed and dull dark green.

HABIT AND GARDEN USE: A rounded, dense shrub with upright, spreading branches, 4'-8' in height and width. Useful massed around entryways and in courtyards where its fragrance can best be appreciated. Makes an informal barrier or screen. Suitable for containers.

NATIVE HABITAT
Korea

HARDINESS ZONE
USDA 4-7
Sunset 1-11, 14-24

HOW TO GROW: Best in well-drained, slightly acid soil with average moisture. Full sun to partial shade. Prune after flowering. Bacterial leaf spot and powdery mildew are sometimes a problem, so look for resistant cultivars.

The flowers are very fragrant.

CULTIVARS AND RELATED SPECIES

'Cayuga' — Abundant flower clusters with pink buds that open to white, waxy flowers; compact habit to 5' high.

'Compactum' — A dwarf form growing 2'-3-1/2' high and wide; good dark green leaves.

V. x 'Mohawk' — Brilliant red flower buds open to light pink. The most fragrant of the viburnums.

Viburnum carlesii

OUTSTANDING FEATURES: Attractive gray-green foliage and summer flowers in shades of purple, pink or white characterize this popular, though not commonly seen, shrub. Leaves are aromatic and tropical-looking. Flowers are borne in terminal spikes, 3"-8" long from late June into September. A great addition for summer flowers.

Chastetree

HABIT AND GARDEN USE: Plant habit is usually rounded in youth, becoming open and more tree-like with age. Left unpruned, plants in the South may reach 15'-20' in height; in the North, plants are often killed back (sometimes to the ground) and thus never attain their full size. Because of their tropical appearance and summer flowers, chastetrees are good choices for planting around swimming pools and patios. They can also be used in mass or included in shrub and mixed borders.

NATIVE HABITAT
Southern Europe to western Asia

HARDINESS ZONE
USDA Zones 6-9
Sunset 4-24

HOW TO GROW: Easily transplanted from containers in spring. Best in full sun and well-drained soil. Pruning, when necessary, should be done in early spring before growth starts; plants can be rejuvenated by cutting to the ground at this time. No serious pests or diseases.

Vitex agnus-castus

CULTIVARS AND RELATED SPECIES
'Alba' —A white-flowered form with 3"-6" spikes.
'Rosea' —A pink-flowered form with pale flowers on 3"-6" spikes.
'Silver Spire' — A very vigorous form with clear, white flowers on 4"-8" spikes.
V. negundo — A closely related species larger than *V. agnus-castus* and more cold-hardy. Individual flower spikes are not so showy as the latter but are borne in greater profusion. Flowers are pale purple to lavender and appear in July and August.

Weigela florida

OUTSTANDING FEATURES: An old-fashioned favorite grown for its spectacular floral display, which begins in late spring and continues into early summer. The 1"-1-1/4" flowers are borne in axillary clusters and range from pure white to pink to red. Some varieties offer mixes of the above colors, as well as yellow. A real showstopper when in flower.

NATIVE HABITAT
Japan

HARDINESS ZONE
USDA 4-8
Sunset 1-11, 14-17

HABIT AND GARDEN USE: Usually densely branched and spreading. Arching branches tend to touch the ground, for an overall rounded habit. Size ranges from 6'-9' tall with an equal or greater spread; however, there are much more compact cultivars. Best used in shrub or mixed borders or massed.

HOW TO GROW: This weigela is easily transplanted from a container or bare root in early spring. It prefers full sun and well-drained soil, although it tolerates a wide range of soil types. Pruning, when necessary, should be done immediately after flowering because this shrub blooms on the previous year's wood. No serious pests or diseases.

CULTIVARS AND RELATED SPECIES

'Bristol Ruby' —Ruby-red flowers borne in abundance. Very hardy.

'Mont Blanc' — Large, pure white, fragrant flowers; considered by some to be the best white.

'Rubigold' — Ruby-red flowers produced on a plant with golden yellow foliage. Leaf color tends to fade with the onset of hot weather.

'Variegata' — Leaves have pale yellow to white edges; flowers are deep rose.

Weigela florida, an old favorite grown for its spectacular floral display.

RECOMMENDED SHRUBS FOR EVERY REGION

MID-ATLANTIC

Hamamelis x *intermedia* 'Jelena'

Bottlebrush Buckeye *Aesculus parviflora*

Red Chokeberry *Aronia arbutifolia*

Common Butterfly Bush *Buddleia davidii*

Buttercup Winterhazel *Corylopsis pauciflora*

Smokebush *Cotinus coggygria*

Slender Deutzia *Deutzia gracilis*

Dwarf Fothergilla *Fothergilla gardenii*

Witchhazel *Hamamelis* x *intermedia* 'Jelena'

Oakleaf Hydrangea *Hydrangea quercifolia*

Virginia Sweetspire *Itea virginica*

MIDWEST

Cornus stolonifera 'Silver and Gold'

Bottlebrush Buckeye *Aesculus parviflora*

Japanese Barberry *Berberis thunbergii*

Red-twig Dogwood *Cornus stolonifera*

Dwarf Fothergilla *Fothergilla gardenii*

Oakleaf Hydrangea *Hydrangea quercifolia*

Japanese Kerria *Kerria japonica*

Bush Cinquefoil *Potentilla fruticosa*

Fragrant Sumac *Rhus aromatica*

Japanese Spirea *Spiraea japonica* 'Alpina'

Korean Spice Viburnum *Viburnum carlesii*

NORTHEAST

Clethra alnifolia

Bottlebrush Buckeye *Aesculus parviflora*

Red Chokeberry *Aronia arbutifolia*

Summersweet *Clethra alnifolia*

Red-twig Dogwood *Cornus stolonifera*

Burning Bush *Euonymus alatus*

Border Forsythia *Forsythia* x *intermedia*

Dwarf Fothergilla *Fothergilla gardenii*

Witchhazel *Hamamelis* x *intermedia*

Common Lilac *Syringa vulgaris*

Bumald Spirea *Spiraea* x *bumalda*

RECOMMENDED SHRUBS

SOUTHEAST

Loropetalum chinense rubrum

Japanese Camellia
Camellia japonica
Fragrant Wintersweet
Chimonanthus praecox
Thorny Elaeagnus
Elaeagnus pungens
Virginia Sweetspire *Itea virginica*
Loropetalum
Loropetalum chinense

Mountain-laurel *Kalmia latifolia*
Heavenly-bamboo
Nandina domestica
Holly Osmanthus
Osmanthus heterophyllus
Cherry-laurel *Prunus laurocerasus*
Indian Hawthorn
Rhaphiolepis indica

SOUTHERN GREAT PLAINS

Potentilla fruticosa 'Hopley's Orange'

Red Chokeberry *Aronia arbutifolia*
Japanese Barberry
Berberis thunbergii
Bird of Paradise
Caesalpinia gilliesii
Flowering Quince
Chaenomeles speciosa
Burning Bush *Euonymus alatus*

Japanese Privet
Ligustrum japonicum
Fraser Photinia *Photinia* x *fraseri*
Bush Cinquefoil
Potentilla fruticosa
Bumald Spirea *Spiraea* x *bumalda*
Tamarisk *Tamarix ramosissima*

ROCKY MOUNTAINS

Tamarix ramosissima

Red Chokeberry *Aronia arbutifolia*
Japanese Barberry
Berberis thunbergii
Flowering Quince
Chaenomeles speciosa
Red-twig Dogwood
Cornus stolonifera
Cranberry Cotoneaster
Cotoneaster apiculatus

Bush Cinquefoil
Potentilla fruticosa
Fragrant Sumac *Rhus aromatica*
Alpine Currant *Ribes alpinum*
Bumald Spirea *Spiraea* x *bumalda*
Tamarisk
Tamarix ramosissima

RECOMMENDED SHRUBS

PACIFIC NORTHWEST

Mahonia 'Arthur Menzies'

Compact Strawberry Tree
Arbutus unedo 'Compacta'
Japanese Camellia
Camellia japonica
Redvein Enkianthus
Enkianthus campanulatus
Spring Heath *Erica carnea*
Oregon Grape-holly
Mahonia lomariifolia

Delavay's Osmanthus
Osmanthus delavayi
Mountain Andromeda
Pieris japonica
Red-flowering Currant *Ribes sanguineum glutinosum*
Sweetbox *Sarcococca hookeriana humilis*
Korean Spice Viburnum
Viburnum carlesii

CALIFORNIA & DESERT SOUTHWEST

Fremontodendron californicum

Compact Strawberry Tree
Arbutus unedo 'Compacta'
Red Bird of Paradise
Caesalpinia pulcherrima
Feathery Cassia *Senna artemisioides*
California Lilac
Ceanothus 'Julia Phelps'
Orchid Rockrose *Cistus x purpureus*

Common Flannel Bush *Fremontodendron californicum*
New Zealand Tea
Leptospermum scoparium
Texas Ranger
Leucophyllum frutescens
Greek Myrtle *Myrtus communis*
Rosemary *Rosmarinus officinalis*

SUBTROPICAL FLORIDA

Pittosporum tobira 'Variegata'

Flowering Maple
Abutilon x *hybridum*
Angel's Trumpet
Brugmansia versicolor
Mexican-orange *Choisya ternata*
Common Gardenia
Gardenia augusta
Japanese Privet
Ligustrum japonicum

Heavenly-bamboo
Nandina domestica
Fraser Photinia *Photinia x fraseri*
Japanese Pittosporum
Pittosporum tobira
Princess Flower
Tibouchina urvilleana
Chastetree *Vitex agnus-castus*

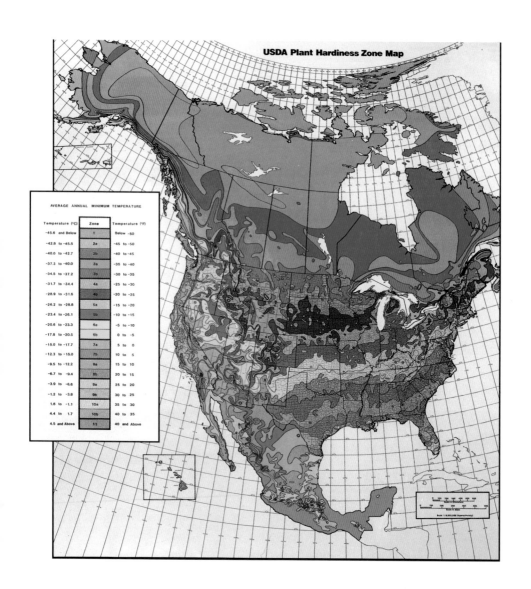

USDA Plant Hardiness Zone Map

AVERAGE ANNUAL MINIMUM TEMPERATURE		
Temperature (°C)	Zone	Temperature (°F)
-45.6 and Below	1	Below -50
-42.8 to -45.5	2a	-45 to -50
-40.0 to -42.7	2b	-40 to -45
-37.3 to -40.0	3a	-35 to -40
-34.5 to -37.2	3b	-30 to -35
-31.7 to -34.4	4a	-25 to -30
-28.9 to -31.6	4b	-20 to -25
-26.2 to -28.8	5a	-15 to -20
-23.4 to -26.1	5b	-10 to -15
-20.6 to -23.3	6a	-5 to -10
-17.8 to -20.5	6b	0 to -5
-15.0 to -17.7	7a	5 to 0
-12.3 to -15.0	7b	10 to 5
-9.5 to -12.2	8a	15 to 10
-6.7 to -9.4	8b	20 to 15
-3.9 to -6.6	9a	25 to 20
-1.2 to -3.8	9b	30 to 25
1.6 to -1.1	10a	35 to 30
4.4 to 1.7	10b	40 to 35
4.5 and Above	11	40 and Above

CONTRIBUTORS

WILLIAM H. FREDERICK, JR. is a landscape architect practicing in Hockessin, Delaware. He is the author of *100 Great Garden Plants* (Knopf, 1975, reprinted by Timber Press, 1986) and *The Exuberant Garden and the Controlling Hand* (Little, Brown, 1992).

KENT GULLICKSON is a horticulturist and garden designer in Oakland, California, specializing in perennials and pond gardens. He has managed nurseries and garden centers throughout northern California.

BOB HAYS is the plant propagator at Brooklyn Botanic Garden. His knowledge of plants and gardens is exceptional.

BOB HYLAND is vice president for horticulture at Brooklyn Botanic Garden. His peripatetic career at Strybing Arboretum and Botanical Gardens in San Francisco and Longwood Gardens in Pennsylvania has acquainted him with plants from around the world.

TED KIPPING is a horticulturist and certified arborist living in San Francisco. An avid plantsman with a complex garden, he travels widely to study, photograph and lecture.

J.C. RAULSTON is professor of horticultural science at North Carolina State University in Raleigh and director of the NCSU Arboretum. His classes and public programs keep plant lovers across the country abreast of new garden plants and how to grow them.

ILLUSTRATION CREDITS

Drawings
by Steve Buchanan

Cover photo and pages 7b,c,d; 20b; 29a,b; 33a; 35b; 38; 41a; 42a; 43b; 44a,b; 45a,b; 47a; 51a; 54a; 56a; 57a,b; 58a,b; 59b; 63b; 65; 70c; 71b; 73a; 74b; 77b; 81; 82b; 83; 85a; 94a; 98b; 99b; 100b; 104b; 105b
by Michael Dirr

Pages 4; 6; 31b; 34a; 41b; 56b; 62; 71a; 75a; 90; 96a; 99a; 103b
by Bob Hyland

Pages 9a,b,c; 11a,b,c; 75b; 102; 104a; 105a,c
by J.C. Raulston

Pages 13; 39a,b
by Larry Albee

Pages 15; 27 left and right; 50; 61a; 73b; 78; 87; 101
by Ken Druse

Pages 17; 34b
by Kent Gullickson

Pages 20a; 28; 32b; 40; 55a; 67; 68; 74a; 79; 80; 85b; 88a; 95; 100a; 103a
by Pamela Harper

Pages 20c; 37; 52; 93; 94b
by Jerry Pavia

Pages 7a; 32a; 48; 51b; 89b; 91; 98a
by E.R. Hasselkus

Pages 1; 33b; 46a,b; 47b; 49; 53a; 54b; 59a; 60; 64; 69; 70a,b; 77a; 89a; 104c
by Harrison Flint

Pages 35a, 53b; 66; 76; 82a; 84; 86; 88b; 92; 97; 103c
by Ellyn Meyers

Pages 31a; 42b; 63a; 96b
by Joanne Pavia

Pages 30; 43a; 55b; 61b
by Bob Hays

Page 72
by John Nemerovski

Pages 27 center; 36
by Mary Irish

American Cottage Gardening

Annuals: A Gardener's Guide

Bonsai: Special Techniques

Culinary Herbs

Dyes from Nature

The Environmental Gardener

Ferns

Garden Photography

The Gardener's World of Bulbs

Gardening for Fragrance

Gardening in the Shade

Gardening with Wildflowers &
    Native Plants

Going Native: Biodiversity
    in Our Own Backyards

Greenhouses & Garden Rooms

Herbs & Cooking

Herbs & Their Ornamental Uses

Hollies: A Gardener's Guide

Indoor Bonsai

Japanese Gardens

The Natural Lawn & Alternatives

Natural Insect Control

A New Look at Vegetables

A New Look at Houseplants

Orchids for the Home & Greenhouse

Ornamental Grasses

Perennials: A Gardener's Guide

Pruning Techniques

Roses

Soils

The Town & City Gardener

Trees: A Gardener's Guide

Water Gardening

The Winter Garden

21st-Century Gardening Series

For centuries, gardens have been islands of beauty and tranquility in an often disorderly, unpredictable world. The late-20th-century garden is also a major arena in the struggle to balance human and ecological needs, one of the great tasks of our time. Brooklyn Botanic Garden's 21st-Century Gardening Series explores the frontiers of ecological gardening. Each volume offers practical, step-by-step tips on creating environmentally sensitive and beautiful gardens for the 1990s and the new century.

TO SUBSCRIBE OR ORDER:

21st-Century Gardening Guides are published quarterly — spring, summer, fall and winter. A four-volume subscription is included in BBG subscribing membership dues of $25 a year. Mail your check to Brooklyn Botanic Garden, 1000 Washington Avenue, Brooklyn, NY 11225.

For information on how to order any of the handbooks listed at left, call (718) 622-4433.